BY MR. FAISAL FAHIM

The most recommended book of MR. FAISAL IS ("**The Bible, the Qu'ran and Science: The Holy Scriptures Examined in the Light of Modern Knowledge: 4 books in 1**") Authored by Mr. Faisal Fahim, Dr. Maurice Bucaille, Dr. Zakir Naik.

AND IT'S AVAILABLE ON AMAZON, www.barnesandnoble.com, www.createspace.com/4459947

Message from the author: My intention is not to criticize any one's beliefe.It's okay to agree or disagree with my book.This entire book is not totally written by me.It is based on a research project done by me.The book is as the title goes.The information is arranged & organized by me & all sources of all documents or information is mentioned inside the book.Purpose of my book is to share the knowledge which is available in many sources & I have mentioned them in the book.Hope you enjoy & share my book. "The greatest creation of god is us.The true race of us the1&only us,all of us the mankind simply1race of humanity. Love is the only antidose of hate.so,love,peace&Godbless for all.knowledge is not only power but it is indeed freedom to speak out the truth of an existence and I will share it to set it free. Thank you for reading my work.God bless planet earth & America"

Introduction of the book:

Allah has promised to keep The Quran same until the Day of Judgment & challenged humans to create another accurate book like Quran & said if you can't, surrender to your lord (the only way of peace& heaven). Quran is word of god & it has the information of past, present& future. God reveled to Prophet Muhammad whatever god wanted to & kept some information only to god by reveling some & not reveling some. But still Quran is 1 great source of information from God.

Do Muslims worship the Mecca? No Muslims bow towards the direction of mecca & worship only 1 God Allah. While praying in a mosque if Muslims will not have a direction they will end up praying facing or towards each other .The Quran & Prophet Muhammad taught us to bow towards the direction of mecca while we only pray & worship Allah. And it's also important for the unity of Muslims.

THE QURAN PROVES WATER CAME FROM ROCKS FROM THE SPACE (by FAISAL)

Scientists don't know for sure. Perhaps the most popular theory says that, shortly after the Earth formed, millions of asteroids and comets, saturated in water, slammed into the planet, releasing their payloads to form Earth's oceans . Scientists are working hard to understand more about what our planet was like billions of years ago, and each new piece of information moves us closer to understanding how Earth's oceans, lakes and rivers came to exist.But the quran already has the answer because the quran is more superior than science & it's the only 100% true book of God's words. Thenceforth were your hearts hardened: They became like a rock and even worse in hardness. For among rocks there are some from which rivers gush forth; others there are which when split asunder send forth water; and others which sink for fear of Allah. And Allah is not unmindful of what ye do. 2:74 al-Baqarah Verse: 74 AL-QURAN.

On the authority of Abu Malik al-Harith bin Asim al-Asharee (may Allah be pleased with him) who said:The Messenger of Allah (peace and blessings of Allah be upon him) said, "Purity is half of iman (faith). 'Al-hamdu lillah (praise be to Allah)' fills the scales, and 'subhan-Allah (how far is Allah from every imperfection) and 'Al-hamdulillah (praise be to Allah)' fill that which is between heaven and earth. And the salah (prayer) is a light, and charity is a proof, and patience is illumination, and the Qur'an is a proof either for you or against you. Every person starts his day as a vendor of his soul, either freeing it or causing its ruin." It was related by Muslim.

God definition By Faisal: God does not born or die. Who has no beginning or end. Does not need to become human, animal or insect to understand his creation. He is the creator who knows what he has created. He is the most wise. So, he knows everything. He feeds everyone, but he doesn't need to eat or sleep or use toilet. True God is the creator who is not part of the creation. So, he has no father, mother, wife or children. He's above all & unique. There's none like him & he's only one, who has no partner & no gender. So, he's the creator of all creation & not part of his or any creation. That is the definition of one true God in Islam which is Allah. Allah has created the humans in a pair of male& female to worship him & in different colors, languages, countries to respect & recognize each other.Tv,watch,computer,phone everything has a purpose. Purpose of us is not just only to eat,poo,have sex&sleep .purpose of life is to obey & worship the creator because humans are the most superior of creation & our purpose is to serve god by praising & praying.No1 is superior whether you are black or white,arab or non arab,male or female .For god everyone is equel.Islam is the only religion that is against racism. Allah is the most just & God judges you by your heart only not by your looks. Islam is an accurate, just & peaceful religion of 1 god creator lord Allah.

In Quran, It says "If you kill one human being it's as
If you have killed the entire of humanity. And if you
save one human being. It's as you saved the entire
of humanity". So, for killing you go to hell, for saving you go to heaven. There was no suicide bombers in the time of prophet Mohammad. Islam believes God created the first humans were Adam & eve without any father & mother. The devil made them eat a fruit that was told by God to not to eat.

And they got poo, but, they were not allowed to poo in heaven. You can eat everything in heaven & you wont get poo & it's a unholy thing you get it when you eat foods on earth & the 1forbidden fruit that was in heaven. So, as punishment God sent them to earth. Adam&Eve were married &having sex for married couples is not sin in islam. All humans are children of Adam & eve. In

Islam from Adam to Moses, to Jesus to Mohammad God sent all of them as messengers prophets & humans to spread the true religion. Because God created Adam & Eve without any father & mother. It means true creator can create everything in any way he wants to, for example If he says something to happen It'll just happen. The same way he made Adam & Eve without being their father & mother plus also having no father & mother. He has the wisdom & power of over everything. Similarity of creating Adam a slight differently he created prophet Jesus as one of the mightiest messengers of God with having just mother without any father. Because God can do anything God can create humans without father & mother as well as having a mother but no father. That's the true miracle & it can only be done by one true creator. And that's the believe of Islam that the true God is Allah who has no partner, no parents, no children, no wife, doesn't born or die, has no image because there's none like him, does not eat but feeds everyone & does not sleep. In Islam the name of prophet Jesus is Isa. And Jesus/Isa did everything with the power of Allah (God). God gave him the power to do it. Who created Jesus as a messenger of God.

Similarly he created Adam, Moses, Abraham, Noah, Isa as Jesus, Mohammad as messengers of peace & Islam towards humanity. And God can't be part of creation. If it's part of creation then it's not the creator or God or Allah. Even in Bible it says Jesus put his head on the floor as Muslims put their head on the floor for praying. 80% of Quran matches with Science & other 20% of Quran the Science does not have the answers because they haven't discovered or improved that much. For example Quran talks

about heaven, hell, & there are aliens. Science has no answer for everything but Quran has all the answers since last 1400 years even when Science had no answers. In the Bible it talks about Prophet Noah & the story goes something like this that the Prophet received a message from God that there would be a flood all over the world. So, he built a big boat & he took some people & a pair of every animals. According to Science there was not a flood which happened all over the world but it happened in a particular part of earth. Quran also tells it

happened in a particular part of the world. Quran also talks about humans are partly formed from father & partly formed from mother. And today Science agrees with it. So, if some one reads Quran & do a scientific research it'll help to understand

what the truth is & what is fiction. Bible says, the world is flat & circle. Scientifically it's not true. A coin is also flat & circle. Quran tells the original shape of earth. Science can't prove any error in Quran but tells errors on Bible. Don't believe it! Do your own research & believe what's logical. Don't ask people but do your own research so, you can believe in true God the creator of all creation but not a creation. Islam also teaches black cumin cures so many diseases without any side effects. The ultimate goal of saitan (Devil) is to take humans towards hell & shirk. Shirk means to associate or include someone with God. True God has no partner, can't compare him with any creation because he has created the creation, how can he be part of what he created? Remember true religion should have all the answers Of humanity & should not have any missing links. Islam believes Quran is 100% words of one creator God Allah. People might think there are 2 types of Muslims Shia & Sunni. But they both have same book Quran. And in Quran there is no Sunni or Shia. Islam is one religion & Quran is the

only one book Of God in Islam. The followers of Islam & Quran are called Muslims. No Muslim is a Muslim unless he beliefs Adam, Moses, Abraham, Jesus, Noah, Mohammad were all messengers of

one God Allah. No Muslim is a good Muslim unless he's a good human being. Islam teaches to live peacefully with people of every religion, race, color, language & nationalities. So we should understand, respect& live peacefully with each other. In the last 100 years to now Islam is the fastest growing religion in the world. That's why some governments & Medias create lies & misconceptions about Islam. Remember, true religion is the one that answers all the questions of humanity. Science can't prove any error in Quran. And true book of God can't have any errors. Muslims believe Torah & Bible were books of God but they have been changed by humans. So,

Quran is the last & final book of God. Quran is only one book but you can find it in all languages. Any one who believes in God should do research on Science, Quran & Bible. Fact is stranger then fiction. The book of God should have all the answers for humanity with no errors & word of God can't have errors!

Question: Does Quran mention that Prophet Muhammad is the last prophet?
Muhammad is not the father of any of your men, but [he is] the messenger of God and seal(last,finish,end,final) of the prophets and God has the knowledge of everything. (Quran 33:40)

Prophet Muhammad (pbuh) is mentioned by name in the Song of Solomon chapter 5 verse 16:

prophet Muhammad (pbuh) mentioned by name in the old testament: Prophet Muhammad (pbuh) is mentioned by name in the Song of Solomon chapter 5 verse 16:"Hikko Mamittakim we kullo Muhammadim Zehdoodeh wa Zehraee Bayna Jerusalem.""His mouth is most sweet: yea, he is altogether lovely. This is my beloved, and this is my friend, O daughters of Jerusalem."In the Hebrew language im is added for respect. Similarely im is added after the name of Prophet Muhammad (pbuh) to make it Muhammadim. In English translation they have even translated the name of Prophet Muhammad (pbuh) as "altogether lovely", but in the Old Testament in Hebrew, the name of Prophet Muhammad (pbuh) is yet present.It's majestic plural noun like Elohim which refers to 1 God only.so Muhammadim also refers to 1 Muhammad even though im can refer also to be plural.(Edited by Faisal)

Was prophet Jesus punished for other peoples sins:No,it was his enemy whose look was turned into the look & face of jesus.jesus was taken alive to heaven by God.jesus will come back and will die on this earth as a human & messenger of allah.from Adam to Moses to Jesus to Mohammad god sent all of them as messengers & they were all muslims.God is the most just .He never does unjust.Every one will be punished for their own sins.God will never punish Jesus or anyone for the sins of others because that's unjust & common sence.God is the most merciful he will forgive whoever he wishes to. But the sinner will have to ask for forgiveness ,beg for it & promise god to not to repeat it again & god will forgive. Pray to god:god you love forgiveness,you are the forgiver I'm a sinner so please forgive me. people judge people .Allah judges you by your heart.

Quran is not a copy of anything & there is no evidence to say such. Statements in Quran are against torah & bible.Torah & bible has so many errors. & according to science 80%of Quran matches with science &other 20%of Quran science doesn't have answers maybe it will take couple of hundred years to find out for sciense. Acording to historians original bible doesn't exist anymore. According to Islam torah&bible were books of Allah but humans have destroyed their originality. So Quran is the last &final word of god Allah &Muhammad is the last&final messenger of Allah. Quran is not copy of anything and its 100% word of god in Islam. According to science torah &bibles statements have errors &Qurans statements are accurate

&word of god is accurate.

QUESTION: WHY WOMEN CAN'T HAVE 4 HUSBANDS?

Answer: If a man has 4 wives &they have a child there would be 1father&that's the husband only. If a woman has 4 husbands &she gives birth it would be confusing to know who is father out of 4.But now with DNA test you can find out. And suddenly all 4 wives want to be a mom. They can go to 1 husband make love, wait couple of more months &finally give birth of their childs.In the same time 4 husbands want to have their own baby with 1 wife & only she can give birth the husbands can't give birth &they don't want their baby in a test tube or other women to give birth except their own married wife. Now they will either kill each other to have 1 to make love with his wife or divorce her or leave her forever or even worst rape & kill her simply creating the most dangerous situation. A man is allowed to marry up to 4 only not 5 or 6.First the rule is to marry only 1 & then if he can do justice&treat all 4 100% equally and of course take her all responsibility meaning can effort her 100% only then he can marry upto 4.Prophet Muhammad said the best of man is the 1 who is the best to his wife. A man asked the prophet who should I do the most favor to 1st he replied your mother the man asked 2nd he replied your mother man asked 3rd he replied your mother, man asked for 4th time he replied your father. The mother has 3times more right then the father. He also said the heaven is in beneath the foot of your mother. A wife's heaven is beneath the foot of her husband. In Quran it says men are like the clothes to their wives &wives are like the clothes to their husbands. It means they are both equal to Allah god even their physical shapes & purpose are different. & clothes were very important things in that time &still are. It's a grace a mercy & a blessing of god Allah that women can give birth and be a mother which man can never do or earn that right & respect &position of a woman in Islam. But in Christianity and Judaism giving birth and having the monthly period or menses was seen as a punishment &a curse from god. In the past they even dared to ask if a woman had a soul? Again the maximum wives a man can have are 4 not anymore. The bible has no restrictions on how many wives or husbands can a person have it's the church's decision to have 1husband&1wife.In Islam a woman can have only 1 husband. For more information search in Google by your own self &believe in the evidence from god the holy Quran which provides peace &protection for humanity. May Allah guide&protect all.No hate only love peace&godbless for all.

The Quran and Modern Science

On Faith, The Holy Quran | by Dr. Maurice Bucaille (Edited by Dr. A. A. Bilal Philips)

EDITOR'S FOREWORD

This booklet by Dr. Maurice Bucaille has been in circulation for the past nineteen years and has been a very effective tool in presenting Islam to non-Muslims as well as introducing Muslims to aspects of the scientific miracle of the Qur'an. It is based on a transcription of a lecture given by

Dr. Bucaille in French. In this reprint, I decided to improve its presentation by simplifying the language and editing the text from an oral format to a pamphlet format. There were also passing references made by the author to material in his book, The Bible, the Qur'an and Science, which needed explanation. I took the liberty of including explanatory portions from his book where more detail was necessary. A few footnotes were also added for clarity and a hadeeth which the author mentioned was replaced due to its inauthenticity. There were also some corrections made to the historical material on the compilation of the Qur'an.

It is my hope that these slight improvements will make this excellent work even more effective in presenting the final revelation of God to mankind.

Dr. Abu Ameenah Bilal Philips

Director/Islamic Information Center Dubai

U.A.E.

May, 1995

INTRODUCTION

On the 9th of November, 1976, an unusual lecture was given at the French Academy of Medicine. Its title was "Physiological and Embryological data in the Qur'an". I presented the study based on the existence of certain statements concerning physiology and reproduction in the Qur'an. My reason for presenting this lecture was because it is impossible to explain how a text produced in the seventh century could have contained ideas that have only been discovered in modern times.

For the first time, I spoke to members of a learned <u>medical</u> society on subjects whose basic concepts they all knew well, but I could, just as easily, have pointed out statements of a scientific nature contained in the Qur'an and other subjects to specialists from other disciplines. Astronomers, zoologists, geologists and specialists in the history of the earth would all have been struck, just as forcibly as medical doctors, by the presence in the Qur'an of highly accurate reflections on natural phenomena. These reflections are particularly astonishing when we consider the history of science, and can only lead us to the conclusion that they are a challenge to human explanation.

There is no human work in existence that contains statements as far beyond the level of knowledge of its time as the Qur'an. Scientific opinions comparable to those in the Qur'an are the result of modern knowledge. In the commentaries to translations of the Qur'an that have appeared in European languages, I have only been able to find scattered and vague references to them. Nor do commentators writing in Arabic provide a complete study of the aspects of the Qur'an that deal with scientific matters. This is why the idea of a comprehensive study of the problem appealed to me. In addition to this, a comparative study of similar data contained in the Bible (Old Testament and Gospels) seemed desirable. Thus, a research project was developed from the comparison of certain passages in the Holy Scriptures of each monotheistic religion with modern scientific knowledge. The project resulted in the publication of a book entitled, The Bible, the Qur'an and Science. The first French edition appeared in May 1976. English and Arabic editions have since been published.

RELIGION AND SCIENCE

There is, perhaps, no better illustration of the close links between Islam and science than the Prophet Muhammad's often-quoted statements:

"Seeking knowledge is compulsory on every Muslim."

"wisdom is the lost property of the believer."

"whoever follows a path seeking knowledge, Allah will make his path to paradise easy."

These statements and many others are veritable invitations to humanity to enrich their knowledge from all sources. It comes as no surprise, therefore, to learn that in Islam religion and science have always been considered as twin sisters and that today, at a time when science has taken such great strides, they still continue to be associated. Nor is it a surprise to learn that certain scientific data are used for the better understanding of the Qur'anic text. What is more, in a century where, for many people, scientific truth has dealt a deathblow to religious belief, it is precisely the discoveries of science that, in an objective examination of the Islamic scripture, have highlighted the supernatural nature of revelation and the authenticity of the religion which it taught.

When all is said and done, scientific knowledge seems, in spite of what many people may say or think, to be highly conducive to reflection on the existence of God. Once we begin to ask ourselves, in an unbiased or unprejudiced way, about the metaphysical lessons to be derived

from some of today's knowledge, (for example our evolving knowledge of the smallest components of matter or the questions surrounding the origin of life within inanimate matter), we indeed discover many reasons for thinking about God. When we think about the remarkable organization presiding over the birth and maintenance of life, it becomes clear that the likelihood of it being the result of chance lessens quite considerably.

As our knowledge of science in the various fields expands, certain concepts must seem increasingly unacceptable. For example, the idea enthusiastically expressed by the recent French winner of the Nobel prize for medicine, that living matter was self-created from simple chemical elements due to chance circumstances. Then from this point it is claimed that living organisms evolved, leading to the remarkably complex being called man. To me, it would seem that the scientific advancements made in understand the fantastic complexity of higher beings provides stronger arguments in favor of the opposite theory: that the existence of an extraordinarily

methodical organization presiding over the remarkable arrangement of the phenomena of life necessitates the existence of a Creator.

In many parts of the Book, the Qur'an, encourages this kind of general reflection but also contains infinitely more precise data which are directly related to facts discovered by modern science. It is precisely this data which exercise a magnetic attraction for today's scientists.

The Qur'an and Science

For many centuries, humankind was unable to study certain data contained in the verses of the Qur'an because they did not possess sufficient scientific means. It is only today that numerous verses of the Qur'an dealing with natural phenomena have become comprehensible. A reading of old commentaries on the Qur'an, however knowledgeable their authors may have been in their day, bears solemn witness to a total inability to grasp the depth of meaning in such verses. I could even go so far as to say that, in the 20th century, with its compartmentalization of ever-increasing knowledge, it is still not easy for the average scientist to understand everything he reads in the Qur'an on such subjects, without having recourse to specialized research. This means that to understand all such verses of the Qur'an, one is nowadays required to have an absolutely encyclopedic knowledge embracing many scientific disciplines.

I should like to stress, that I use the word science to mean knowledge which has been soundly established. It does not include the theories which, for a time, help to explain a phenomenon or a series of phenomena, only to be abandoned later on in favor of other explanations. These newer explanations have become more plausible thanks to scientific progress. I only intend to deal with comparisons between statements in the Qur'an and scientific knowledge which are not likely to be subject to further discussion. Wherever I introduce scientific facts which are not yet 100% established, I will make it quite clear.

There are also some very rare examples of statements in the Qur'an which have not, as yet, been confirmed by modern science. I shall refer to these by pointing out that all the evidence available today leads scientists to regard them as being highly probable. An example of this is the

statement in the Qur'an that life has an aquatic origin ("And I created every living thing out of water" Qur'an, 21:30).

These scientific considerations should not, however, make us forget that the Qur'an remains a religious book par excellence and that it cannot be expected to have a scientific purpose per se. In the Qur'an, whenever humans are invited to reflect upon the wonders of creation and the numerous natural phenomena, they can easily see that the obvious intention is to stress Divine Omnipotence. The fact that, in these reflections, we can find allusions to data connected with scientific knowledge is surely another of God's gifts whose value must shine out in an age where scientifically based atheism seeks to gain control of society at the expense of the belief in God. But the Qur'an does not need unusual characteristics like this to make its supernatural nature felt. Scientific statements such as these are only one specific aspect of the Islamic revelation which the Bible does not share.

Throughout my research I have constantly tried to remain totally objective. I believe I have succeeded in approaching the study of the Qur'an with the same objectivity that a doctor has when opening a file on a patient. In other words, only by carefully analyzing all the symptoms can one arrive at an accurate diagnosis. I must admit that it was certainly not faith in Islam that first guided my steps, but simply a desire to search for the truth. This is how I see it today. It was mainly the facts which, by the time I had finished my study, led me to see the Qur'an as the divinely-revealed text it really is.

AUTHENTICITY OF QUR'AN

Before getting to the essence of the subject, there is a very important point which must be considered: the authenticity of the Qur'anic text.

It is known that the text of the Qur'an was both recited from memory, during the time it was revealed, by the Prophet and the believers who surrounded him, and written down by designated scribes among his followers. This process lasted for roughly twenty-three years during which many unofficial copies were made. An official copy was made within one year after the Prophet's death at the instruction of Caliph Abu Bakr.

Here we must note a highly important point. The present text of the Qur'an benefited in its original preparation from the advantage of having its authenticity cross-checked by the text recited from memory as well as the unofficial written texts. The memorized text was of paramount importance at a time when not everyone could read and write, but everybody could memorize. Moreover, the need for a written record was included in the text of the Qur'an itself. The first five verses of chapter al-'Alaq, which happen to constitute the first revelation made to the Prophet (S), express this quite clearly:

"Read: In the name of your Lord who created. Who created man from a clinging entity. Read! Your Lord is the most Noble, Who taught by the pen. Who taught man what he did not know." Qur'an, 96:1-5

These are surely words in "praise of the pen as a means of human knowledge", to use Professor Hamidullah's expression.

Then came the Caliphate of 'Uthman (which lasted from the twelfth to the twenty-fourth year following Muhammad's death). Within the first two years of Caliph 'Uthman's rule, seven official copies were reproduced from the official text and distributed throughout a large area of the world which had already come under Islamic rule. All unofficial copies existing at that time were destroyed and all future copies were made from the official seven copies.

In my book, The Bible, the Qur'an and Science, I have quoted passages from the Qur'an which came from the period prior to the Hijrah (the Prophet's emigration from Makkah to Madeenah in the year 622) and which allude to the writing of the Qur'an before the Prophet's departure from Makkah.

There were, moreover, many witnesses to the immediate transcription of the Qur'anic revelation.

Professor Jacques Berque has told me of the great importance he attaches to it in comparison with the long gap separating the writing down of the Judeo-Christian revelation from the facts and events which it relates. Let us not forget that today we also have a number of manuscripts of the first written versions of the Qur'an which were from a time period very close to the time of revelation.

I shall also mention another fact of great importance. We shall examine statements in the Qur'an which today appear to merely record scientific truth, but of which men in former times were only able to grasp the apparent meaning. In some cases, these statements were totally incomprehensible. It is impossible to imagine that, if there were any alterations to the texts, these obscure passages scattered throughout the text of the Qur'an, were all able to escape human manipulation. The slightest alteration to the text would have automatically destroyed the remarkable coherence which is characteristic to them. Change in any text would have prevented us from establishing their total conformity with modern knowledge. The presence of these statements spread throughout the Qur'an looks (to the impartial observer) like an obvious hallmark of its authenticity.

The Qur'an is a revelation made known to humans in the course of twenty-three years. It spanned two periods of almost equal length on either side of the Hijrah. In view of this, it was natural for reflections having a scientific aspect to be scattered throughout the Book. In a study, such as the one we have made, we had to regroup the verses according to subject matter, collecting them chapter by chapter.

How should they be classified? I could not find any indications in the Qur'an suggesting any particular classification, so I decided present them according to my own personal one.

It would seem to me, that the first subject to deal with is Creation. Here it is possible to compare the verses referring to this topic with the general ideas prevalent today on the formation of the Universe. Next, I divided up verses under the following general headings: Astronomy, the Earth, the Animal and Vegetable Kingdoms, Humans, and Human Reproduction in particular. Furthermore, I thought it useful to make a comparison between Qur'anic and Biblical narrations on the same topics from the point of view of modern knowledge. This has been done in the cases of Creation, the Flood and the Exodus. The reason that these topics were chosen is that knowledge acquired today can be used in the interpretation of the texts.

CREATION OF THE UNIVERSE

From an examination of creation as described in the Qur'an, an extremely important general concept emerges: The Qur'anic narration is quite different from the Biblical narration. This idea contradicts the parallels which are often wrongly drawn by Western authors to emphasize the resemblance between the two texts. To stress only the similarities, while silently ignoring the obvious dissimilarities, is to distort reality. There is, perhaps, a reason for this.

- When talking about creation, there is a strong tendency in the West to claim that Muhammad copied the general outlines mentioned in the Qur'an from the Bible.

- Certainly it is possible to compare the six days of creation as described in the Bible, plus an extra day for rest on God's Sabbath, with this verse from chapter al-A'raaf.

"Your Lord is God who created the heavens and the earth in six days." Qur'an, 7:54

However, it must be pointed out that modern commentators stress the interpretation of the Arabic word ayyaam, (one translation of which is 'days'), as meaning 'long periods' or 'ages' rather than periods of twenty-four hours.

What appears to be of fundamental importance to me is that, in contrast to the narration contained in the Bible, the Qur'an does not lay down a sequence for creation of the earth and heavens. It refers both to the heavens before the earth and the earth before the heavens, when it talks of creation in general, as in this verse of chapter Taa Haa:

"(God) who created the earth and heavens above." Qur'an, 20:4

In fact, the notion derived from the Qur'an is one of a parallelism in the celestial and terrestrial evolutions. There are also basic pieces of information concerning the existence of an initial gaseous mass (dukhaan) which are unique to the Qur'an. As well as descriptions of the elements which, although at first were fused together (ratq), they subsequently became separated (fatq). These ideas are expressed in chapters Fussilat and al-Anbiyaa:

"God then rose turning towards the heaven when it was smoke" Qur'an, 41:11

"Do the disbelievers not see that the heavens and the earth were joined together, then I split them apart?" Qur'an, 21:30

According to modern science, the separation process resulted in the formation of multiple worlds, a concept which appears dozens of times in the Qur'an. For example, look at the first chapter of the Qur'an, al-Faatihah:("Praise be to God, the Lord of the Worlds." Qur'an, 1:1). These Qur'anic references are all in perfect agreement with modern ideas on the existence of primary nebula (galactic dust), followed by the separation of the elements which resulted in the formation of galaxies and then stars from which the planets were born. Reference is also made in the Qur'an to an intermediary creation between the heavens and the earth, as seen in chapter al-Furqaan:

"God is the one who created the heavens, the earth and what is between them…" Qur'an, 25:59

It would seem that this intermediary creation corresponds to the modern discovery of bridges of matter which are present outside organized astronomical systems.

This brief survey of Qur'anic references to creation clearly shows us how modern scientific data and statements in the Qur'an consistently agree on a large number of points. In contrast, the successive phases of creation mentioned in the Biblical text are totally unacceptable. For

example, in Genesis 1:9-19 the creation of the earth (on the 3rd day) is placed before that of the heavens (on the 4th day). It is a well known fact that our planet came from its own star, the sun. In such circumstances, how could anyone claim that Muhammad, the supposed author of the Qur'an, drew his inspiration from the Bible. Such a claim would mean that, of his own accord, he corrected the Biblical text to arrive at the correct concept concerning the formation of the Universe. Yet the correct concept was reached by scientists many centuries after his death.

ASTRONOMY

Whenever I describe to Westerners the details the Qur'an contains on certain points of astronomy, it is common for someone to reply that there is nothing unusual in this since the Arabs made important discoveries in the field of astronomy long before the Europeans. But, this is a mistaken idea resulting from an ignorance of history. In the first place, science developed in the Arab World at a considerable time after the Qur'anic revelation had occurred. Secondly, the scientific knowledge prevalent at the highpoint of Islamic civilization would have made it impossible for any human being to have written statements on the heavens comparable to those in the Qur'an. The material on this subject is so vast that I can only provide a brief outline of it here.

The Sun and Moon.

Whereas the Bible talks of the sun and the moon as two lights differing only in size, the Qur'an distinguishes between them by the use of different terms: light (noor) for the moon, and lamp (siraaj) for the sun.

"Did you see how Allah created seven heavens, one above the other, and made in them the moon a light and the sun a lamp?" Qur'an, 78:12-13

The moon is an inert body which reflects light, whereas the sun is a celestial body in a state of permanent combustion producing both light and heat.

Stars and Planets

The word 'star' (najm) in the Qur'an (86:3) is accompanied by the adjective thaaqib which indicates that it burns and consumes itself as it pierces through the shadows of the night. It was much later discovered that stars are heavenly bodies producing their own light like the sun.

In the Qur'an, a different word, kawkab, is used to refer to the planets which are celestial bodies that reflect light and do not produce their own light like the sun.

"We have adorned the lowest heaven with ornaments, the planets." Qur'an, 37:6

Orbits Today, the laws governing the celestial systems are well known. Galaxies are balanced by the position of stars and planets in well-defined orbits, as well as the interplay of gravitational forces produced by their masses and the speed of their movements. But is this not what the Qur'an describes in terms which have only become comprehensible in modern times. In chapter al-Ambiyaa we find:

"(God is) the one who created the night, the day, the sun and the moon. Each one is traveling in an orbit with its own motion." Qur'an, 21:33

The Arabic word which expresses this movement is the verb yasbahoon which implies the idea of motion produced by a moving body, whether it is the movement of one's legs running on the ground, or the action of swimming in water. In the case of a celestial body, one is forced to translate it, according to its original meaning, as 'to travel with its own motion.'

In my book, The Bible, The Qur'an and Science, I have given the precise scientific data corresponding to the motion of celestial bodies. They are well known for the moon, but less widely known for the sun.

The Day and Night

The Qur'anic description of the sequence of day and night would, in itself, be rather commonplace were it not for the fact that it is expressed in terms that are today highly appropriate. The Qur'an uses the verb kawwara in chapter az-Zumar to describe the way the night 'winds' or 'coils' itself around the day and the day around the night.

"He coils the night upon the day and the day upon the night." Qur'an, 39:5

The original meaning of the verb kis to coil a turban around the head. This is a totally valid comparison; yet at the time the Qur'an was revealed, the astronomical data necessary to make this comparison were unknown. It is not until man landed on the moon and observed the earth spinning on its axis, that the dark half of the globe appeared to wind itself around the light and the light half appeared to wind itself around the dark.

The Solar Apex

The notion of a settled place for the sun is vividly described in chapter Yaa Seen of the Qur'an:

"The sun runs its coarse to a settled place That is the decree of the Almighty, the All Knowing." Qur'an, 36:38

"Settled place" is the translation of the word mustaqarr which indicates an exact appointed place and time. Modern astronomy confirms that the solar system is indeed moving in space at a rate of 12 miles per second towards a point situated in the constellation of Hercules (alpha lyrae) whose exact location has been precisely calculated. Astronomers have even give it a name, the solar apex.

Expansion of the Universe Chapter ath-Thaariyaat of the Qur'an also seems to allude to one of the most imposing discoveries of modern science, the expansion of the Universe.

"I built the heaven with power and it is I, who am expanding it." Qur'an, 51:47

The expansion of the universe was first suggested by the general theory of relativity and is supported by the calculations of astrophysics. The regular movement of the galactic light towards the red section of the spectrum is explained by the distancing of one galaxy from another. Thus, the size of the universe appears to be progressively increasing.

Conquest of Space

Among the achievements of modern science is the "conquest" of space which has resulted in mans journey to the moon. The prediction of this event surely springs to mind when we read the chapter ar-Rahmaan in the Qur'an:

"O assembly of Jinns and men, if you can penetrate the regions of the heavens and the earth, then penetrate them! You will not penetrate them except with authority."

Qur'an, 55:33

Authority to travel in space can only come from the Creator of the laws which govern movement and space. The whole of this Qur'anic chapter invites humankind to recognize God's beneficence.

GEOLOGY

Let us now return to earth to discover some of the many amazing statements contained in Qur'anic reflections about our own planet. They deal, not only with the physical phenomena observed here on earth, but also with details concerning the living organisms that inhabit it.

As in the case of everything we have discussed so far, we shall see that the Qur'an also expresses concepts in the field of geology that were way ahead of those current at the time of its revelation.

At this point, we must ask ourselves the following question: How could an uneducated man in the middle of the desert accurately tackle so many and such varied subjects at a time when mythology and superstition reigned supreme? How could he so skillfully avoid every belief that was proven to be totally inaccurate many centuries later?

Water Cycle

The verses dealing with the earthly systems are a case in point. I have quoted a large number of them in my book, The Bible, The Qur'an and Science, and have paid special attention to those that deal with the water cycle in nature. This is a topic which is well known today. Consequently, the verses in the Qur'an that refer to the water cycle seem to express ideas that are now totally self-evident. But if we consider the ideas prevalent at that time, they appear to be based more on myth and philosophical speculation than on observed fact, even though useful practical knowledge on soil irrigation was current at that period.

Let us examine, for example, the following verse in chapter az-Zumar:

"Have you not seen that Allah sent rain down from the sky and caused it to penetrate the ground and come forth as springs, then He caused crops of different colors to grow…" Qur'an, 39:21

Such notions seem quite natural to us today, but we should not forget that, not so long ago, they were not prevalent. It was not until the sixteenth century, with Bernard Palissy, that we gained the first coherent description of the water cycle. Prior to this, people believed that the waters of the oceans, under the effect of winds, were thrust towards the interior of the continents. They then returned to the oceans via the great abyss, which, since Plato's time was called the Tartarus. In the seventeenth century, great thinkers such as Descartes still believed in this myth. Even in the nineteenth century there were still those who believed in Aristotle's theory that water was condensed in cool mountain caverns and formed underground lakes that fed springs. Today, we know that it is the infiltration of rain water into the ground that is responsible for this. If one compares the facts of modern hydrology with the data found in numerous verses of the Qur'an on this subject, one cannot fail to notice the remarkable degree of agreement between the two.

Mountains

In geology, modern science has recently discovered the phenomenon of folding which formed the mountain ranges. The earth's crust is like a solid shell, while the deeper layers are hot and fluid, and thus inhospitable to any form of life. It has also been discovered that the stability of mountains is linked to the phenomenon of folding. The process of mountain formation by folding drove the earth's crust down into the lower layers and provided foundations for the mountains.

Let us now compare modern ideas with one verse among many in the Qur'an that deals with this subject. It is taken from chapter an-Naba':

"Have We not made the earth an expanse and the mountains stakes?"

Qur'an, 78:6-7

Stakes (awtaad), which are driven into the ground like those used to anchor a tent, are the deep foundations of geological folds.

Here, as in the case of all the other topics presented, the objective observer cannot fail to notice the absence of any contradiction to modern knowledge.

BIOLOGY More than anything else, I was struck by statements in the Qur'an dealing with living things, both in the animal and vegetable kingdoms, especially with regard to reproduction. We should really devote much more time to this subject, but, due to the limited scope of this presentation, I can only give a few examples.

I must once again stress the fact that it is only in modern times that scientific progress has made the hidden meaning of some Qur'anic verses comprehensible to us. Numerous translations and commentaries on the Qur'an have been made by learned men who had no access to modern scientific knowledge. It is for this reason that scientists find some of their interpretations unacceptable.

There are also other verses whose obvious meanings are easily understood, but which conceal

scientific meanings which are startling, to say the least. This is the case of a verse in chapter al-Ambiyaa, a part of which has already been quoted:

"Do the unbelievers not realize that the heavens and the earth were joined together,

then I clove them asunder and I made every living thing out of water. Will they still not believe?" Qur'an, 21:30

This is a dramatic affirmation of the modern idea that the origin of life is aquatic.

Botany

Progress in botany at the time of Muhammad (S) was not advanced enough in any country for scientists to know that plants have both male and female parts. Nevertheless, we may read the following in the chapter Taa Haa:

"(God is the One who) sent down rain from the sky and with it brought forth a variety of plants in pairs." Qur'an, 20:53

Today we know that fruit comes from plants that have sexual characteristics even when they come from unfertilized flowers, like bananas. In the chapter ar-Ra'd we read the following:

"… and of all fruits (God) placed (on the earth) two pairs." Qur'an, 13:3

Physiology

In the field of physiology, there is one verse which appears extremely significant to me. One thousand years before the discovery of the blood circulatory system, and roughly thirteen centuries before it was determined that the internal organs were nourished by the process of digestive , a verse in the Qur'an described the source of the constituents of milk, in conformity with scientific facts.

To understand this verse, it must first be known that chemical reactions occur between food and enzymes in the mouth, the stomach and the intestines releasing nutrients in molecular form which are then absorbed into the circulatory system through countless microscopic projections of the intestinal wall called villi. Blood in the circulatory system then transports the nutrients to all the organs of the body, among which are the milk-producing mammary glands.

This biological process must be basically understood, if we are to understand a verse in the Qur'an which has for many centuries given rise to commentaries that were totally incomprehensible.

Today it is not difficult to see why! This verse is taken from the chapter an-Nahl:

"Verily, in cattle there is a lesson for yon. I give you drink from their insides, coming from a conjunction between the digested contents (of the intestines) and the blood, milk pure and pleasant for those who drink it." Qur'an, 16:66

The constituents of milk are secreted by the mammary glands which are nourished by the product of food digestion brought to them by the bloodstream. The initial event which sets the whole process in motion is the conjunction of the contents of the intestine and blood at the level of the intestinal wall itself.

This very precise concept is the result of the discoveries made in the chemistry and physiology of the digestive system over one thousand years after the time of Prophet Muhammad (S).

EMBRYOLOGY

There are a multitude of statements in the Qur'an on the subject of human reproduction which constitute a challenge to the embryologist seeking a human explanation for them. It was only after the birth of the basic sciences which contributed to our knowledge of biology and the invention of the microscope, that humans were able to understand the depth of those Qur'anic statements. It was impossible for a human being living in the early seventh century to have accurately expressed such ideas. There is nothing to indicate that people in the Middle-East and Arabia knew anything more about this subject than people living in Europe or anywhere else. Today, there are many Muslims, possessing a thorough knowledge of the Qur'an and natural sciences, who have recognized the amazing similarity between the verses of the Qur'an dealing with reproduction and modern scientific knowledge.

I shall always remember the comment of an eighteen-year-old Muslim, brought up in Saudi Arabia, commenting on a reference to human reproduction as described in the Qur'an. He pointed to the Qur'an and said, "This book provides us with all the essential information on the subject. When I was at school, my teachers used the Qur'an to explain how children were born. Your books on sex-education are a bit late on the scene!"

If I were to spend as long on all the details of reproduction contained in the Qur'an, as the subject merits, this pamphlet would become a book. The detailed linguistic and scientific explanations I have given in The Bible, The Qur'an and Science are sufficient for the person who does not speak Arabic nor know much about embryology to be able to understand the meaning of such verses in the light of modern science in more depth.

It is especially in the field of embryology that a comparison between the beliefs present at the time of the Qur'an's revelation and modern scientific data, leaves us amazed at the degree of agreement between the Qur'an's statements and modern scientific knowledge. Not to mention the total absence of any reference in the Qur'an to the mistaken ideas that were prevalent around the world at the time.

Fertilization

Let us now isolate, from all these verses, precise ideas concerning the complexity of the semen and the fact that an infinitely small quantity is required to ensure fertilization. In chapter al-Insaan the Qur'an states:

"Verily, I created humankind from a small quantity of mingled fluids." Qur'an, 76:2

The Arabic word nutfah has been translated as "small quantity". It comes from the verb meaning 'to dribble, to trickle' and is used to describe what remains in the bottom of a bucket which has been emptied. The verse correctly implies that fertilization is performed by only a very small volume of liquid.

On the other hand, mingled fluids (amshaaj) has been understood by early commentators to refer to the mixture of male and female discharges. Modern authors have corrected this view and note that the sperm is made up of various components.

When the Qur'an talks of a fertilizing fluid composed of different components, it also informs us that human progeny will be formed from something extracted from this liquid. This is the meaning of the following verse in chapter as-Sajdah:

"Then He made [man's] offspring from the essence of a despised fluid."
Qur'an, 32:8

The Arabic word translated by the term 'essence' is sulaalah which means 'something extracted, the best part of a thing'. In whatever way it is translated, it refers to part of a whole. Under normal conditions, only one single cell, spermatozoon, out of over 50 million ejaculated by a man during sexual intercourse will actually penetrate the ovule.

Implantation

Once the egg has been fertilized in the fallopian tube, it descends to lodge itself inside the uterus. This process is called the 'implantation of the egg'. Implantation is a result of the development of villosities, which, like roots in the soil, draw nourishment from the wall of the uterus and make the egg literally cling to the womb. The process of implantation is appropriately described in several verses by the word 'alaq, which is also the title of the chapter in which one of the verses appears:

"God fashioned humans from a clinging entity." Qur'an, 96:2

I do not think there is any reasonable translation of the word 'alaq other than to use it in its original sense. It is a mistake to speak of a 'blood clot' here, which is the term Professor Hamidullah uses in his translation. It is a derivative meaning which is not as appropriate in this context.

Embryo

The evolution of the embryo inside the maternal uterus is only briefly described, but the description is accurate, because the simple words referring to it correspond exactly to fundamental stages in its growth. This is what we read in a verse from the chapter al-Mu'minoon:

"I fashioned the clinging entity into a chewed lump of flesh and I fashioned the chewed flesh into bones and I clothed the bones with intact flesh." Qur'an, 23:14

The term 'chewed flesh' (mudghah) corresponds exactly to the appearance of the embryo at a certain stage in its development.

It is known that the bones develop inside this mass and that they are then covered with muscle. This is the meaning of the term 'intact flesh' (lahm).

The embryo passes through a stage where some parts are in proportion and others out of proportion with what is later to become the individual. This is the obvious meaning of a verse in the chapter al-Hajj, which reads as follows:

"I fashioned (humans) a clinging entity, then into a lump of flesh in proportion and out of proportion." Qur'an, 22:5.

Next, we have a reference to the appearance of the senses and internal organs in the chapter as-Sajdah:

"… and (God) gave you ears, eyes and hearts." Qur'an, 32:9

Nothing here contradicts today's data and, furthermore, none of the mistaken ideas of the time have crept into the Qur'an. Throughout the Middle Ages there were a variety of beliefs about human development based on myths and speculations which continued for several centuries after the period. The most fundamental stage in the history of embryology came in 1651 with Harvey's statement that "all life initially comes from an egg". At that time, when science had benefited greatly from the invention of the microscope, people were still arguing about the respective roles of the egg and spermatozoon. Buffon, the great naturalist, was one of those in favor of the egg theory. Bonnet, on the other hand, supported the theory of 'the ovaries of Eve', which stated that Eve, the mother of the human race, was supposed to have had inside her the seeds of all human beings packed together one inside the other.

BIBLE, QUR'AN AND SCIENCE

We have now come to the last subject I would like to present in this short pamphlet: it is the comparison between modern knowledge and passages in the Qur'an that are also referred to in the Bible.

Creation

We have already come across some of the contradictions between scripture and science regarding the creation of the universe. When dealing with that topic, I stressed the perfect agreement between modern knowledge and verses in the Qur'an, and pointed out that the Biblical narration contained statements that were scientifically unacceptable. This is hardly surprising if we are aware that the narration of the creation contained in the Bible was the work of priests living in the sixth century BC, hence the term 'sacerdotal' (priestly) narration is officially used to refer to it. The narration seems to have been conceived as the theme of a sermon designed to exhort people to observe the Sabbath. The narration was constructed with a definite end in view, and as Father de Vaux (a former head of the Biblical School of Jerusalem) has noted, this end was essentially legalist in character.

The Bible also contains a much shorter and older narration of Creation, the so-called 'Yahvist' version, which approaches the subject from a completely different angle. They are both taken from Genesis, the first book of the Pentateuch or Torah. Moses is supposed to have been its author, but the text we have today has undergone many changes.

The sacerdotal narration of Genesis is famous for its whimsical genealogies, that go back to Adam, and which nobody takes very seriously. Nevertheless, such Gospel authors as Matthew and Luke have reproduced them, more or less word-for-word, in their genealogies of Jesus. Matthew goes back as far as Abraham, and Luke to Adam. These writings are scientifically unacceptable, because they set a date for the age of the world and the time humans appeared on Earth, which most definitely contradicts what modern science has firmly established. The Qur'an, on the other hand, is completely free of dates of this kind.

Earlier on, we noted how perfectly the Qur'an agrees with modern ideas on the formation of the Universe. On the other hand, the Biblical narration of primordial waters is hardly, nor is the creation of light on the first day before the creation of the stars which produce this light; the existence of an evening and a morning before the creation of the earth; the creation of the earth on the third day before that of the sun on the fourth; the appearance of beasts of the earth on the sixth day after the appearance of the birds of the air on the fifth day, although the former came first. All these statements are the result of beliefs prevalent at the time this text was written and do not have any other meaning.

Age of the Earth As for the Biblical genealogies which form the basis of the Jewish calendar and assert that today the world is 5738 years old, these are hardly admissible either. Our solar system may well be four and a quarter billion years old, and the appearance of human beings on earth, as we know him today, may be estimated in tens of thousands of years, if not more. It is absolutely essential, therefore, to note that the Qur'an does not contain any such indications as to the age of the world, and that these are specific to the Biblical text.

The Flood

There is a second highly significant subject of comparison between the Bible and the Qur'an; descriptions of the deluge. In actual fact, the Biblical narration is a fusion of two descriptions in which events are related differently. The Bible speaks of a universal flood and places it roughly

300 years before Abraham.

According to what we know of Abraham, this would imply a universal cataclysm around the twenty-first or twenty-second century BC This story would be untenable, in view of presently available historical data. How can we accept the idea that, in the twenty-first or twenty-second century BC, all civilization was wiped off the face of the earth by a universal cataclysm, when we know that this period corresponds, for example, to the one preceding the Middle Kingdom in Egypt, at roughly the date of the first Intermediary period before the eleventh dynasty? It is historically unacceptable to maintain that, at this time, humanity was totally wiped out. None of the preceding statements is acceptable according to modern knowledge. From this point of view, we can measure the enormous gap separating the Bible from the Qur'an.

In contrast to the Bible, the narration contained in the Qur'an deals with a cataclysm that is limited to Noah's people. They were punished for their sins, as were other ungodly peoples. The Qur'an does not fix the cataclysm in time. There are absolutely no historical or archaeological objections to the narration in the Qur'an.

The Pharaoh

A third point of comparison, which is extremely significant, is the story of Moses, and especially the Exodus from Egypt of the Hebrews. Here I can only give a highly compressed account of a study on this subject that appears in my book. I have noted the points where the Biblical and Qur'anic narrations agree and disagree, and I have found points where the two texts complement each other in a very useful way.

Among the many hypotheses, concerning the historical time-frame occupied by the Exodus in the history of the pharaohs, I have concluded that the most likely is the theory which makes Merneptah, Ramesses II's successor, the pharaoh of the Exodus. The comparison of the data contained in the Scriptures with archeological evidence strongly supports this hypothesis. I am pleased to be able to say that the Biblical narration contributes weighty evidence leading us to situate Moses in the history of the pharaohs. Moses was probably born during the reign of Ramesses II. Biblical data. are therefore of considerable historical value in the story of Moses. A medical study of the mummy of Merneptah has yielded further useful information on the p35 possible causes of this pharaoh's death. The fact that we possess the mummy of this pharaoh is one of paramount importance. The Bible records that pharaoh was engulfed in the sea, but does not give any details as to what subsequently became of his corpse. The Qur'an, in chapter Yoonus, notes that the body of the pharaoh would be saved from the waters:

"Today I will save your dead body so that you may be a sign for those who come after you." Qur'an, 10:92

A medical examination of this mummy, has, shown that the body could not have stayed in the water for long, because it does not show signs of deterioration due to prolonged submersion. Here again, the comparison between the narration in the Qur'an and the data provided by modern knowledge does not give rise to the slightest objection from a scientific point of view.

Such points of agreement are characteristic of the Qur'anic revelation. But, are we throwing the Judeo-Christian revelation into discredit and depriving it of all its intrinsic value by stressing the faults as seen from a scientific point of view? I think not because the criticism is not aimed at the text as a whole, but only at certain passages. There are parts of the Bible which have an undoubted historical value. I have shown that in my book, The Bible, The Qur'an and Science, where I discuss passages which enable us to locate Moses in time.

The main causes which brought about such differences as arise from the comparison between the Holy Scriptures and modern knowledge is known to modern scholars. The Old Testament constitutes a collection of literary works produced in the course of roughly nine centuries and which has undergone many alterations. The part played by men in the actual composition of the texts of the Bible is quite considerable.

The Qur'anic revelation, on the other hand, has a history which is radically different. As we have already seen, from the moment it was first commto humans, it was learnt by heart and written down during Muhammad's own lifetime. It is thanks to this fact that the Qur'an does not pose any problem of authenticity.

A totally objective examination of the Qur'an, in the light of modern knowledge, leads us to recognize the agreement between the two, as has already been noted on repeated occasions throughout this presentation.

It makes us deem it quite unthinkable for a man of Muhammad's time to have been the author of such statements, on account of the state of knowledge in his day. Such considerations are part of what gives the Qur'anic revelation its unique place among religious and non-religious texts, and forces the impartial scientist to admit his inability to provide an explanation based solely upon materialistic reasoning.Such facts as I have had the pleasure of exposing to you here, appear to represent a genuine challenge to human explanation leaving only one alternative: the Qur'an is undoubtedly a revelation from God.

What non Muslim scholars say about Prophet Muhammad (PBUH)

During the centuries of the crusades, all sorts of slanders were invented against the Prophet Muhammad (p)2. However, with the birth of the modern age, marked with religious tolerance and freedom of thought, there has been a great change in the approach of Western authors in their delineation of his life and character.

The West, however, has yet to go a step forward to

discover the greatest reality about Muhammad (p); that is his being the true and the last Prophet of God for all humanity.

Despite all its objectivity and enlightenment, there has been no sincere and objective attempt by the West to understand the Prophethood of Muhammad (p). It is so strange that very glowing tributes are paid to him for his integrity and achievement but his claim of being the Prophet of God is rejected explicitly or implicitly. It is here that a searching of the heart is required, and a review of the so-called objectivity is needed. The following glaring facts from the life of Muhammad (p) have been furnished to facilitate an unbiased, logical and objective decision regarding his Prophethood.

Up to the age of forty, Muhammad (p) was not known as a statesman, a preacher or an orator. He was never seen discussing the principles of metaphysics, ethics, law, politics, economics or sociology. No doubt he possessed an excellent character and charming manners and was known to be highly cultured. Yet there was nothing so deeply striking and so radically extraordinary in him that would make men expect something great and revolutionary from him in the future. But when he came out of the Cave of Hira, with a new message, he was completely transformed. .Is it possible for a person known to possess an upright and unblemished character, to suddenly turn an impostor. and claim to be the Prophet of God?. It is well known that his claim invited the rage of his people, and marked the beginning of a long, arduous struggle. One might ask: .for what reason did he suffer all those hardships?His people offered to accept him as their King and to lay all the riches of the land at his feet if only he would leave the preaching of his message. But he turned down their alluring offers and continued to preach in the face of insults, social boycott and even physical assault. Furthermore, had he come with a design of rivalry with the Christians and the Jews, why should he have believed in Jesus Christ and Moses and other Prophets of God (peace be upon them), which is a basic requirement of faith without which no one could be a Muslim?

It is well known that Muhammad (p) was unlettered and had led a very uneventful life before he announced his mission to the world at the age of forty. Is it not an incontrovertible proof of his Prophethood, that despite being unlettered, all of Arabia stood in awe and wonder when he began preaching his message, and was bewitched by the wonderful eloquence of his message? The whole legion of Arab poets, preachers and orators of the highest caliber failed to bring forth the equivalent of the Qur.an, which remains inimitable to this day. And above all, how could he then pronounce truths of scientific nature contained in the Qur.an that no human being could possibly have discovered at that time

Last, but not the least, why did he lead a hard life even after gaining power and authority? The words he uttered while dying were: .We the community of the Prophets are not inherited. Whatever we leave is for charity.
As a matter of fact, Muhammad (p), is the last link of Prophets sent in different lands and times since the beginning of the human life on earth.

If greatness of purpose, smallness of means, and astounding results are the three criteria of human genius, who could dare to compare any great man in modern history with Muhammad? The most famous men created arms, laws and empires only. They founded, if anything at all, no more than material powers which often crumbled away before their eyes. This man moved not only armies, legislations, empires, peoples and dynasties, but millions of men in one-third of the then inhabited world; and more than that, he moved the altars, the gods, the religions, the ideas, the beliefs and souls... His forbearance in victory, his ambition, which was entirely devoted to one idea and in no manner striving for an empire; his endless prayers, his mystic conversations with God, his death and his triumph after death; all these attest not to an impostor but to a firm conviction which gave him the power to restore a dogma. This dogma was twofold, the unity of God and the immateriality of God; the former telling what God is, the latter telling what God is not; the one overthrowing false gods with the sword, the other starting an idea with the words.

Philosopher, orator, apostle, legislator, warrior, conqueror of ideas, restorer of rational dogmas, of a cult without images; the founder of twenty terrestrial empires and of one spiritual empire, that is Muhammad. As regards all standards by which human greatness may be measured, we may well ask, is there any man greater than he?[Lamartine, Histoire de la Turquie, Paris 1854 Vol. II, pp. 276-77.]

It is not the propagation but the permanency of his religion that deserves our wonder; the same pure and perfect impression that he engraved at Mecca and Medina is preserved, after the revolutions of twelve centuries by the Indian, the African and the Turkish proselytes of the Koran... The Mahometans have uniformly withstood the temptation of reducing the object of their faith and devotion to a level with the senses and imagination of man. I believe in One God and Mahomet the Apostle of God., is the simple and invariable profession of Islam. The intellectual image of the Deity has never been degraded by any visible idol; the honors of the prophet have never transgressed the measure of human virtue; and his living precepts have restrained the gratitude of his disciples within the bounds of reason and religion.[Edward Gibbon and Simon Ocklay, History of the Saracen Empire, London 1870, p. 54.]

He was Caesar and Pope in one; but he was Pope without Popes pretensions, Caesar without the legions of Caesar: without a standing army, without a bodyguard, without a palace, without a fixed revenue; if ever any man had the right to say that he ruled by the right divine, it was Mohammad, for he had all the power without its instruments and without its supports.[Bosworth Smifu, Mohammad and Mohammadanism. London 1874, p. 92.]

.It is impossible for anyone who studies the life and character of the great Prophet of Arabia, who knows how he taught and how he lived, to feel anything but reverence for that mighty Prophet, one of the great messengers of the Supreme. And although in what I put to you I shall say many things which may be familiar to many, yet I myself feel whenever I re-read them, a new way of admiration, a new sense of reverence for that mighty Arabian teacher.[Annie Besant, The Life and Teachings of Muhammad, Madras 1932, p.4]

His readiness to undergo persecutions for his beliefs, the high moral character of the men who believed in him and looked up to him as leader, and the greatness of his ultimate achievement all argue his fundamental integrity. To suppose Muhammad an impostor raises more problems than it solves. Moreover, none of the great figures of history is so poorly appreciated in the West as Muhammad.[W. Montgomery, Mohammad at Mecca, Oxford, 1953, p. 52.]

Muhammad, the inspired man who founded Islam, was born about A.D. 570 into an Arabian tribe that worshipped idols. Orphaned at birth, he was always particularly solicitous of the poor and needy, the widow and the orphan, the slave and the downtrodden. At twenty he was already a successful businessman, and soon became director of camel caravans for a wealthy widow. When he reached twenty-five his employer, recognizing his merit, proposed marriage. Even though she was fifteen years older, he married her, and as long as she lived remained a devoted husband. Like almost every major prophet before him, Muhammad fought shy of serving as the transmitter of God.s word, sensing his own inadequacy. But the angel commanded Read.. So far as we know, Muhammad was unable to read or write, but he began to dictate those inspired words which would soon revolutionize a large segment of the earth; .There is one God.

In all things Muhammad was profoundly practical. When his beloved son Ibrahim died, an eclipse occurred, and rumors of God.s personal condolence quickly arose. Whereupon Muhammad is said to have announced, An eclipse is a phenomenon of nature. It is foolish to attribute such things to the death or birth of a human being..

At Muhammad.s own death an attempt was made to deify him, but the man who was to become his administrative successor killed the hysteria with one of the noblest speeches in religious history: If there are any among you who worshipped Muhammad, he is dead. But if it is God you worshipped, He lives forever..
[James A. Michener, Islam The Misunderstood Religion., In the Reader.s Digest (American Edition) for May 1955, pp. 68-70.]

[Source : WAMY3 Series on Islam]

1. The 100: A Ranking of the Most Influential Persons in History, New York: Hart Publishing Company, Inc., 1978, p. 33.
2. (p) here stands for .peace be upon him3. World Assembly of Muslim Youth

**Surah Al-Fatiha (The Opening) al Quran)In the name of Allah, the Beneficent, the Merciful Praise be to Allah, Lord of the Worlds,The Beneficent, the Merciful.Owner of the Day of Judgment,Thee (alone) we worship; Thee (alone) we ask for help.Guide us on the 36
straight path,
The path of those whom Thou hast favored;Not (the path) of those who earn Thine anger nor of those who go astray.
(1 : 1-7)**

Mistakes in the Torah proved by the discoveries of modern science
The Torah has many verses, which contradict modern scientific facts.
These contradictions indicate that the Torah is not the word of Allah
(S.W.) who is far from errors and ignorance of science facts that man discovered later. Allah (S.W.), the Omniscient, would not tell in his
book except the truth. He has a complete perfect knowledge of every
thing in the universe.
- The Torah mentions the story of the creation in Genesis, where it
talks about the creation of the universe in six earthly days consisting

of mornings and evenings.

According to the biblical order, on the first day, He created the earth, the light, the darkness, and the water. On the second day, He created the sky when He put a firmament between water and water, and on the third day, the water gathered under the firmament, the land appeared and the herbs and grass grew.

On the fourth day, He created the sun, the moon, and the stars that above the firmament (the sky), and on the fifth day, He created the marine animals and the birds. On the sixth day, He created Adam and the wild animals, and finished the creation on that day. (See Genesis 1: 1 - 31)

Scientists note that the order and the directing of the story of the beginning of the universe are rejected by modern science that Allah (S.W.) gave to humanity. If these books were from Allah (S.W.), they would not contain these continuous errors.

Genesis talks about six earthly days consisting of days and nights (***And there was evening and there was morning***), and the seventh day was the Sabbath, on which the Creator rested (God Almighty is far above that). It is well known scientifically that the creation of the universal happened during periods of millions of years. Allah (S.W.) is right when He mentions in the Holy Quran the difference between His days and human days. "***Verily, a Day in the sight of thy Lord is like a thousand years of your reckoning.***"
(Holy Quran, Surah 22, Al-Hajj – 47)

Scientists say that the Earth's surface took millions of years to cool down and became suitable for living. Genesis says that the water appeared on earth on its first day, then the appearance of the plants on its third, and the animals on the fourth and the fifth days.

The biblical order of the appearance of the creations contradicts the findings of geologic history. The presence of water on the face of the earth on the first day contradicts the scientific theory that the earth and the universe were gas at the beginning of creation. In addition, the plants cannot appear before the existence of the sun, and the marine animals and birds were not before wild animals.

Scientifically, saying that the creation of the earth was before the creation of the sun and the stars (on the fourth day) is wrong. Moreover, the appearance of the night and the day for three days, without the sun is surprising!

In addition, saying that the appearance of plants was three days before man is wrong. Scientific discoveries tell us that the presence of vegetations was millions of years before the presence of man. The majority of the objections about this story of creation are in father Devoux's criticism of Genesis.

- Among the scientific observations on the Torah, is that it speaks at length about the age of the founding fathers from Adam to Abraham. It makes the birth of Abraham in the twentieth century from the beginning of human existence on earth, specifically in the year 1948 of the creation of the universe and the appearance of man on earth. There is no historical accurate information about the period between Abraham and Jesus, but historians estimated it to be eighteen centuries, depending on the biblical sources. Therefore, the appearance of Christ was thirty-eight centuries after the creation of Adam.

1 - The Torah, the Gospel, and the Quran and Science, Maurice Bocaille, pp 44 – 51, A study on the Torah and the Gospel, Kamel Saafan, pp179, Readings in the Holy Bible, Abderrahim Mohamad, Vol.2, pp 182 - 183

According to the Hebrew date, the year (2000) is equal to the year 5761 of the creation of the universe; therefore, the biblical information makes human life on earth no more than six thousand years. This contradicts the scientific data, which consider the biblical Informations are full of errors or written by men not God. Science has proved the existence of civilizations five thousand years before the birth of Jesus.

Archaeologists believe that there was a bloody war between the north and the south of Egypt in 4042 BCE, and won by the people of the Egyptian Delta. However, their victory was not decisive, as the Egyptian civilization recorded history started with the first family, which ruled Egypt between 3400 to 3200 BCE, and there is much that that had not been recorded.

Archaeologists also found human-made things that belong to more than five thousand years BCE, and the mission of Cairo University found traces of humans in the Fayoum region belong to tens of thousands of earlier years.

Encyclopedia Britannica states that the human traces in Palestine belong to two hundred thousand years. Donald Jean said in 1979, *"The human presence on earth was four million years ago"*.

Allah (S.W.) is right when He affirms in the Holy Quran that humanity started long centuries ago. ***"(Pharaoh) said: "What then is the condition of previous generations?" He replied: "The knowledge of that is with my Lord, duly recorded: my Lord never errs, nor forgets."*** (Holy Quran, Surah 20, Ta Ha – 51 - 52) ***"As also 'Ad and Thamud, and the Companions of the Rass, and many a generation between them."*** (Holy Quran, Surah 25, Al Furqan – 38) ***"Has not the story reached you, (O people!), of those who (went) before you of the people of Noah, and 'Ad, and Thamud? - And of those who (came) after them? None knows them but Allah."*** (Holy Quran, Surah 14, Ibrahim – 38)

2 - The Torah, the Gospel, and the Quran and Science, Maurice Bocaille, pp 20, A study on the Torah and the Gospel, Kamel Saafan, pp179

- In addition, there are many things the Torah mentions that are contrary to the scientifically well established facts. It mentions that the rabbit is one of the ruminant animals! It says, ***"Nevertheless these ye shall not eat of them that chew the cud, or of them that have the hoof cloven: the camel, and the hare, and the coney; because they chew the cud but part not the hoof, they are unclean unto you"*** (Deuteronomy 14: 7)

- It also mentions that the serpent was punished by eating or licking the soil, (See Genesis 3:14), as in the Book of Micah. ***"They shall lick the dust like a serpent; like crawling things of the earth"*** (Micah 7: 17) All types of snakes that scientifically classified eat insects and reptiles and others, they never eat or lick soil.
- Leviticus speaks of legendary birds that have four legs - some leap, and some walk -, which do not exist except in legendary fiction. It says, ***"All winged creeping things that go upon all fours are an abomination unto you. Yet these may ye eat of all winged creeping things that go upon all fours, which have legs above their feet, wherewith to leap upon the earth. Even these of them ye may eat... But all winged creeping things, which have four feet, are an abomination unto you."*** (Leviticus 11: 20-23) No archaeological reports or other information states that something like this was on the face of earth one day.
- Among the scientific errors also is what the Book of Genesis mentions (30: 37-43). It claims that Jacob's sheep produced, and the color of the production was different from the color of the parents. He prepared some rods of fresh poplar and almond and pealed white streaks on them. Seeing these peeled rods, the sheep craved, and brought forth ring streaked, speckled, and spotted sheep. If this was true, the sheep's production in spring would be green, but this mistake is man made errors & is contrary to what scientists know about genes and genetic codes.so, it can't be word of the lord.
- The Book of Genesis mentions the strangest birth story, namely the story of Tamar, the adulterous, delivering the twins from Judas, her father-in-law and the father of her husbands. ***"And it came to pass in the time of her travail, that, behold, twins were in her womb. And it came to pass, when she travailed, that one put out a hand: and the midwife took and bound upon his hand a scarlet thread, saying, This came out first. And it came to pass, as he drew back his hand, that, behold, his brother came out: and she said, Wherefore hast thou made a breach for thyself? Therefore his name was called Perez. And afterward came out his brother, that had the scarlet thread upon his hand: and his name was called Zerah"*** (Genesis 38: 27-30) The first-born put his hand out of his mother's womb, which is unusual during the birth process. However, the baby wanted to affirm his right of being the first-born child, and the midwife understood him, and bound upon his hand a scarlet thread.

Then a stranger thing, which medical theories cannot explain, happened. The first-born gave a space so his twin brother so he could come out into the world, and then he (whom his hand had a scarlet thread) followed him. This story cannot be accepted scientifically, and append it to the stories of the elderly better than append it to Allah's (S.W.) word and revelation.
- The Book of Job gives a strange vision of the creation of the fetus. It is poured in a template as pouring milk, then clots in the middle of this template, as the clotting milk transformed into cheese. This has

nothing to do whatsoever with what scientists know about the stages of the creation of the fetus.

Addressing Allah (S.W.), the Book of Job says, *"Remember, I beseech thee, that thou hast fashioned me as clay; And wilt thou bring me into dust again? Hast thou not poured me out as milk, And curdled me like cheese? Thou hast clothed me with skin and flesh, And knit me together with bones and sinews."* (Job 10: 9 -11)

- The Torah claims that the earth has pillars, has corners, and it is flat, approving the scientific mainstream during the time of the writing. It says, *"The sun also arises, and the sun goes down, and haste to its place where it arises."* (Ecclesiastes 1: 5) The writer did not know neither that the earth is spherical, nor that it spins on its axis to create the sunrise and sunset.

The author of that verse was not Allah (S.W.) the Omniscient, who says, **"He created the heavens and the earth in true (proportions): He makes the Night overlap the Day, and the Day overlap the Night: He has subjected the sun and the moon (to His law)"** (Holy Quran, Surah 39, Az-Zumar – 5)

Describing Allah (S.W.), the Torah says that He is *"That shaketh the earth out of its place, And the pillars thereof tremble"*. (Job 9: 6) The holy books' writers confirmed this misconception. They claimed that Allah (S.W.) said to Job, *"Where were you when I put the earth on its base? Say, if you have knowledge. By whom were its measures fixed? Say, if you have wisdom; or by whom was the line stretched out over it? On what were its pillars based, or who laid its corner-stone"* (Job 38: 4-6), and the Book of Samuel says. *"For the pillars of the earth are Lord's, and he hath set the world upon them."* (1Samuel 2: 8).

The New Testament confirms this naive and wrong perception of the earth; it is flat, with pillars, and with four corners, in some verses, which I will mention them in their place of this series.

Ecclesiastes speaks about the water cycle on earth and why the sea would not be full, although much water is poured into it from rivers. It mentions that the seawater goes back again to the springs of the rivers, so the sea would not be full. It says, *"All the rivers run into the sea, yet the sea doth not overflow: unto the place from whence the rivers come, they return, to flow again "*. (Ecclesiastes 1: 7)

Finally, the Torah ratifies that humans have the ability of bringing the souls of the dead, and tells that this actually happened. The sorcerer was able to bring Prophet Samuel's spirit to King Saul, and explained the talk between them. (See1Samuel 28: 3-20) This is close to witchcraft and myth more than anything else.

These errors and others testify that this book is not the word of Allah (S.W.), if it is from Allah (S.W.) it would not contain these errors, which today's young students know, let alone the scientists. The word of Allah (S.W.) does not err, nor teach people lies or error.

<u>Killing innocent human</u> is a major sin in Islam & Islam is against terrorism. prophet

Muhammad said no one has the right to burn anything only god has the right to burn someone which is in hell. Love peace for all. May god bless &save us all.

Thomas Carlyle, struck by this philosophy of life writes "and then also Islam-that we must submit to God; that our whole strength lies in resigned submission to Him, whatsoever he does to us, the thing he sends to us, even if death and worse than death, shall be good, shall be best; we resign ourselves to God." The same author continues "If this be Islam, says Goethe, do we not all live in Islam?" Carlyle himself answers this question of Goethe and says "Yes, all of us that have any moral life, we all live so. This is yet the highest wisdom that heaven has revealed to our earth."

Evolution in the Holy Quran:

It is mentioned in the quran 1400 years ago even before scientists found the genetic similarities of monkeys ,apes & humans. what scientists have found is true but their opinion of the theory of evolution is wrong. Quran is word of god & it has the information of past,present& future.God reveled to prophet Muhammad whatever god wanted to & kept some information only to god by reveling some & not reveling some.But still quran is 1 great source of information from God. Because of their constant defiance and blasphemy of GOD Almighty's Divine and Holy Words, some bad Jews were transformed into swines and apes during Prophet Moses (peace be upon him) times:but not the good one's & definitely not all jews okay.

"Say: "Shall I point out to you something much worse than this, (as judged) by the treatment it received from God? those who incurred the curse of God and His wrath, those of whom some He transformed into apes and swine, those who worshipped evil;- these are (many times) worse in rank, and far more astray from the even path!" (The Noble Quran, 5:60)"

First 2 of the 10 Commandments

I am the Lord thy God,Thou shalt have no other gods before me.

Thou shalt not make unto thee any graven images.

SURAT AL IKHLAS (MAKKAH)
1) Say he is Allah one & only
(2) Allah, the eternal; absolute
3) He begets not, nor is he begotten
(4) And there is none like unto him (Al-Quran)

The original quran is 100% accurate in the Arabic language & its 1 only.But in English there are couple of translations of the same 1 arabic quran.so if some 1 wants to understand the quran properly he should read it in couple of translations of the same 1 arabic quran & learn some Arabic to understand the quran more accurately.

Quran is not a copy of anything & there is no evidence to say such.statements in quran are against torah&bible.torah & bible has so many errors. & acording to sciense 80%of quran matches with sciense&other 20%of quran siense doesn't have answers maybe it will take couple of hundred years to find out for siense.acording to historians original bible doesn't exist anymore. Acording to islam torah&bible were books of allah but humans have destroyed their originality. so quran is the last &final word of god allah &Muhammad is the last&final messenger of allah. Quran is not copy of anything and its 100% word of god in islam.

According to sciense torah &bibles statements have errors &Qurans statements are accurate &word of god is accurate.

Reasons why you should not blame religion for the acts of some people

Can u blame Christianity for the acts of crusades, holocaust,& because some priests rapes children inside the churches or because some Christian leaders dropped a nuclear bomb on japan. Or they did these horrible acts like these: George W. Bush Jr. - Christian, Turned Iraq war into a religious war by saying "god told him to invade Iraq", increase taxes on the middle class and poor, cut taxes for the rich.
Nazism – Christians Adolph Hitler - Christian/Catholic Newt Gingrich – Christian Inquisitions - Christian Ugandan Christians Salem Witch burnings – Christian Waco Texas – Christian Jones Town - ChristianSan Diego Heaven's Gate – Christian Serbians – Christian Skin Heads – Christians   IRA (Irish Republican Army) – Christian Iron Guard – Christian Westboro Baptist church – ChristiansChristian Tsarist Russia – Christian The Crusades - Christian & Catholic The Troubles - Catholic & Christian The Holocaust - Catholic & Christian The Book burnings - Catholic & Christian The heretic burnings – Christian Backing of the institution of slavery!!!!----

The answer is No no no and noooooo okay!!! its not the fault of Christianity but rather these are the faults of some bad people who did bad things & its as simple as that okay.Remember the good the bad the ugly exists in every thing or kind of people.Similarly blaming the religion islam for the acts of some few muslims who are evil terrorists is also wrong.Yes there are some bad bad bad people among muslims but again good people do good things & bad people do bad things.Im not denying or defending them because there are evil &good people among all religions & even atheists . It's as simple as that. 99% of muslims are not terrorists.&the bad muslims Or terrorists do not represent the true islam period. suppose some 1 has a very good expensive car or maybe it's the best car in the world.Now the owner starts driving the car he starts drinking & he hits women children & starts killing innocent people.Now is this is a fault of the car? No of course not it's the fault of the driver.over here im representing the driver as a bad muslim or u can say a terrorist & its not the cars fault that the driver misused it so here the expensive good car is islam.my point is don't blame Islam or Christianity or any other religion for the acts of some evil people. Remember the good the bad the ugly exists in every thing or kind of people.Islam is 1 of the most beautiful religion in the world but unfortunately its blamed for the actions of few evil terrorists.& also be aware that there are many rumors, lies & false information & accusations that exists in the western world & some European countries against islam & prophet mohammad.unfortunately some people believe in these false lies which has been spread by crusades, some media, some parts of governments & some bad rich anti Islam politicians to create misconceptions against islam & prophet mohammad only to stop spreading the truth about islam.

Philosopher, orator, apostle, legislator, warrior, conqueror of ideas, restorer of rational dogmas, of a cult without images; the founder of twenty terrestrial empires and of one spiritual empire, that is Muhammad. As regards all standards by which human greatness may be measured, we may well ask, is there any man greater than he?[Lamartine, Histoire de la Turquie, Paris 1854 Vol. II, pp. 276-77.]He was Caesar and Pope in one; but he was Pope without Popes pretensions, Caesar without the legions of Caesar: without a standing army, without a bodyguard, without a palace, without a fixed revenue; if ever any man had the right to say that he ruled by the right divine, it was Mohammad, for he had all the power without its instruments and without its supports.[Bosworth Smifu, Mohammad and Mohammadanism. London 1874, p. 92.] At Muhammad.s own death an attempt was made to deify him, but the man who was to become his administrative successor killed the hysteria with one of the noblest speeches in religious history: If there are any among you who worshipped Muhammad, he is dead. But if it is God you worshipped, He lives forever.[James A. Michener, Islam The Misunderstood Religion] And for atheists in the history the world wars didn't cause by religion.And good people do good things & bad people do bad things.The good the bad the ugly is part of human nature.

The Piercing Star and Black holes

The holy Quran is word of god. The Almighty revealed it to his final prophet to humanity. When prophets were inviting their people to the truth,

God endowed them with miracles to convince their people. Moses was given a miracle that excelled magic and dazzled magicians in ancient Egypt. Jesus was given a miracle that excelled medicine and he could cure people from incurable diseases. The only people who could see these miracles are the ones who were there. Because the prophet Muhammad was the final prophet his miracle had to be continuous and immortal, this immortal miracle is the holy Quran itself.At the age of revealing the holy Quran Arabs were excelled in poetry and prose, so the holy Quran challenged them by its eloquence. Now miracles of the holy Quran appeared in the scientific signs mentioned in a lot of verses, these verses indicate to scientific facts which have been discovered since only few decades, So humanity must know that the holy Quran is the word of Allah.One of the scientific signs mentioned in the holy Quran is the piercing star. (1) The Almighty says in the beginning of surat Al-Tarek: (By the heaven and the Tarik (The Knocker) * Ah, what will tell thee what the Tarik (The knocker) is! * The piercing Star!) (Quran 86:1-3)These verses speak about a star which has two significant features. The first one is that it is a piercing star the other is that it knocks something hard enough to make sound. Allah (SWT) in these verses coupled His oath by heaven regarding its greatness with the piercing star which means that there is a relationship between both. The question now is How do these verses indicate to black holes? Black holes are the most violent and mysterious phenomenon in the sky. Black holes are the evolutionary endpoints of stars at least 10 to 15 times as massive as the Sun. If a star that massive or larger undergoes a supernova explosion, it may leave behind a fairly massive burned out stellar remnant. With no outward forces to oppose gravitational forces, the remnant will collapse in on itself. The star eventually collapses to the point of zero volume and infinite density, creating what is known as a "singularity". As the gravitational field is so powerful that nothing, including light, can escape its pull, the black hole has a one-way surface, called the event

horizon, into which objects can fall, but out of which nothing can come out. At this we have to clarify very important point – which causes confusion to a lot of people- that we must distinguish between the event horizon of the black hole at which any matter or light can not escape and the point at which the matter of the exploded star is collapsed. If the sun become a black hole it will have an event horizon with radius about 3 km but all its matter will be condensed in a point at the center of the black hole.(General relativity describes a black hole as a region of empty space with a point like singularity at the center and an event horizon at the outer edge). (2)

The piercing star describes the matter of star condensed in singularity and the hole of empty space caused by this condensed matter.

The verse indicates to the black hole The verse describes this phenomenon as the piercing star and this is more accurate description because the matter of the collapsed star which is condensed in singularity is the reason of forming the black hole. So the star itself still there condensed causing the existence of this empty space called black hole. When you describe this phenomenon as a black hole you actually are describing only the empty space but if you describe it the piercing star, then you are describing the matter of star condensed in singularity and the hole of empty space caused by this matter.*Types of black holes* There are two main types of black holes the first one is the stellar black holes and the second is actually the biggest and greatest phenomenon in the sky, it is the supermassive black holes. This confirms to us why the oath of the piercing star in the holy Quran is great enough to be coupled with the oath of heaven regarding its greatness.*The properties of supermassive black holes* The most significant feature of the supermassive black hole is its mass which exceed all limits of imagination if you know that the mass of stellar black holes can reach 30 times solar mass, the mass of a supermassive black hole can reach ten billion times solar mass. It is formed also as result of collapse of the matter of supermassive star at the beginning of formation of galaxies, so the piercing star which is condensed in a tiny volume causing this supermassive black hole is considered to be the most massive star in the universe. (3)*The story begins with Quasars* It has got along time for scientists to discover the supermassive black holes and the beginning was the discovery of quasars. The QUASi-stellAR radio source (quasar) is a powerfully energetic and distant active galactic nucleus. The most luminous quasars radiate at a rate that can exceed the output of average galaxies, equivalent to one trillion (1012) suns. Scientist for along time have wondered how does a quasar produce such tremendous luminosity despite its distance from us which reaches billions of light years and the answer came from the most violent thing in sky it is the supermassive black hole. The huge luminosity of quasars results from the accretion discs of central supermassive black holes, which can convert on the order of 10% of the mass of an object into energy as compared to 0.7% for the p-p chain nuclear fusion process that dominates the energy production in sun-like stars. (4)

 The huge luminosity of quasars results from the accretion discs of central supermassive black holes

The cosmic knocks resulted from supermassive black holes The mentioned verses (By the heaven and the Tarik (The Knocker) * Ah, what will tell thee what the Tarik (The knocker) is! * The piercing Star!) (Quran 86:1-3) stated that the piercing star which we explained its relation to supermassive black hole has another significant feature as the verses called it Al-Tarik (The knocker) so how does the piercing star and the resulted supermassive black hole knock?Part of the matter of accretion disk rotating supermassive black hole which is 81
about to fall in the supermassive black hole is re-emitted as Relativistic jets which are extremely powerful twin jets of plasma being shot along the axis of spin of the accretion disk having a velocity approaching the speed of light. This jet knocks hardly and strongly any thing in its way and for long distances.And due to the movement of this plasma jet it knocks the interstellar and the intergalactic medium producing real sound waves.

A real jet of plasma produced by a supermassive black hole in the galaxy (M87) recorded by Hubel space telescope. It

knocks every thing in its way for a distance (5000 light years).

In Sept. 9, 2003: Astronomers using NASA's Chandra X-ray Observatory have found, for the first time, sound waves from a supermassive black hole. This supermassive black hole resides in the Perseus cluster of galaxies located 250 million light years from Earth. The "note" is the deepest ever detected from any object in our Universe. (5)

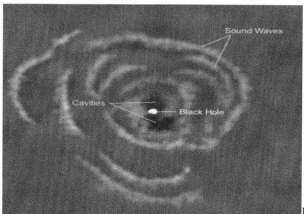

Real sound waves resulted from jets knocking the intergalactic medium. **Now imagine how great the miracle in the verses is. The piercing star and the resulted supermassive black hole knocks the intergalactic medium with relativistic jets and as result of this knocking real sound is produced.(By the heaven and the Tarik (The Knocker) * Ah, what will tell thee what the Tarik (The knocker) is! * The piercing Star!) (Quran 86:1-3)** *The piercing star and heaven* **Allah (SWT) in these verses coupled His oath by heaven regarding its greatness with the piercing star which means that there is a fundamental relationship between this type of stars and all what we see in the sky from stars and galaxies.** *The piercing star is in the core of all galaxies* **Quasar and related supermassive black holes have been associated to a type of galaxies called active galaxies, but the other type of galaxies called inactive galaxies which includes our galaxy the Milky way are thought for a long time to have no supermassive black holes in their cores, but from about two decades scientists have found a method to determine the existence of supermassive black hole by determining the velocities of stars close to the galactic nuclei and they were surprised when they found a supermassive black hole in all galaxies.**

What remained is to know is there a supermassive black hole in our galaxy the Milky way or not. In 2003 American astrophysicist Andrea Ghez and its teamwork (UCLA) and by using high spatial resolution imaging techniques have confirmed the existence of a supermassive black hole in our own galaxy. (6)The image is now complete each galaxy has its own supermassive black hole, but why there are active galaxies and inactive ones. The answer of this question related to the development of galaxies.

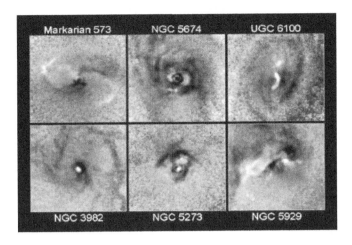

There is a supermassive black hole in each galaxy *Supermassive black hole and the birth of galaxies* Scientists have found a relationship between the velocity of stars at the edges of galaxies and the mass of the supermassive black holes in the core of these galaxies and because the distance between them are very large so this relation formed in a pervious time, the time of galaxy birth as it thought that the galaxies are formed when a huge cloud of gas is collapsed at its core forming supermassive black hole which start to feed on the neighboring gas forming a quasar. This quasar triggers the formation of new stars in the entire galaxy so a new active galaxy is formed, but with time the gas start to get far from the supermassive black hole so it has nothing to feed on and the active galaxy converts to inactive one.

So science today makes a relation between the piercing star and all what wee see in the sky from stars and galaxies. For this reason Allah (SWT) in these verses coupled His oath by heaven regarding its greatness with the piercing star which means that there is a fundamental relationship between this type of stars and all what we see in the sky from stars and galaxies.(By the heaven and the Tarik (The Knocker) * Ah, what will tell thee what the Tarik (The knocker) is! * The piercing Star!) (Quran 86:1-3)

References (1) Dr. Zagloul El-Naggar 2001. Al-Ahram 12, 14 (6, 20 /8 /2001).
(2) http://www.physics.hku.hk/~nature/CD/regular_e/lectures/chap17.html
(3) http://en.wikipedia.org/wiki/Supermassive_black_hole
(4) http://imagine.gsfc.nasa.gov/docs/science/know_l1/active_galaxies.html
(5) http://science.nasa.gov/headlines/y2003/09sep_blackholesounds.htm
(6) http://www.astro.ucla.edu/~ghezgroup/gc/index.shtml

Universe   By: Chem. Gamal Abdel-Nasser

THE 7 EARTHS

The Sunnah of Prophet Muhammad is the second revealed source of Islam. Like the Quran, it contains scientific information unavailable 1400 years ago. From these miracles is the "seven" earths, mentioned by the Prophet in several of his sayings. From them are the following two: Hadith 1 It was narrated on the authority of Abu Salamah that a dispute arose between him and some other people (about a piece of land). When he told Aisha (the Prophet's wife) about it, she said, 'O Abu Salamah! Avoid taking the land unjustly, for the Prophet said: "Whoever usurps even one span of land of somebody, its depth through the seven earths will be collared to his neck." (Saheeh Al-Bukhari, 'Book of Oppression.')Hadith 2 Salim narrated on the authority of his father that the Prophet said: "Whoever takes a piece of land of others unjustly, he will sink down the seven earths on the Day of Resurrection." (Saheeh Al-Bukhari, 'Book of Oppression.')The aforementioned hadith prohibits oppression in general, especially the taking of a piece of land belonging to others unjustly. What might the seven earths refer to?Studies in geology have proven that the earth is composed of seven zones, identified from the inner to the outer layers as follows: (1) The Solid Inner Core of Earth: 1.7% of the Earth's mass; depth of 5,150 - 6,370 kilometers (3,219 - 3,981 miles) The inner core is solid and unattached to the mantle, suspended in the molten outer core. It is believed to have solidified as a result of pressure-freezing which occurs to most liquids when temperature decreases or pressure increases. (2) The Liquid Outer core: 30.8% of Earth's mass; depth of 2,890 - 5,150 kilometers (1,806 - 3,219 miles)The outer core is a hot, electrically conducting liquid within which convective motion occurs. This conductive layer combines with Earth's rotation to create a dynamo effect that maintains a system of electrical currents known as the Earth's magnetic field. It is also responsible for the subtle jerking of Earth's rotation. This layer is not as dense as pure molten iron, which indicates the presence of lighter elements. Scientists suspect that about 10% of the layer is composed of sulfur and/or oxygen because these elements are abundant in the cosmos and dissolve readily in molten iron.(3) The "D" Layer: 3% of Earth's mass; depth of 2,700 - 2,890 kilometers (1,688 - 1,806 miles) This layer is 200 to 300 kilometers (125 to 188 miles) thick and represents about 4% of the mantle-crust mass. Although it is often identified as part of the lower mantle, seismic discontinuities suggest the "D"

layer might differ chemically from the lower mantle lying above it. Scientists theorize that the material either dissolved in the core, or was able to sink through the mantle but not into the core because of its density.

(4) Lower Mantle: 49.2% of Earth's mass; depth of 650 - 2,890 kilometers (406 - 1,806 miles)

The lower mantle contains 72.9% of the mantle-crust mass and is probably composed mainly of silicon, magnesium, and oxygen. It probably also contains some iron, calcium, and aluminum. Scientists make these deductions by assuming the Earth has a similar abundance and proportion of cosmic elements as found in the Sun and primitive meteorites.

(5) Middle Mantle (Transition region): 7.5% of Earth's mass; depth of 400 - 650 kilometers (250-406 miles)

The transition region or mesosphere (for middle mantle), sometimes called the fertile layer, contains 11.1% of the mantle-crust mass and is the source of basaltic magmas. It also contains calcium, aluminum, and garnet, which is a complex aluminum-bearing silicate mineral. This layer is dense when cold because of the garnet. It is buoyant when hot because these minerals melt easily to form basalt which can then rise through the upper layers as magma.(6) Upper Mantle: 10.3% of Earth's mass; depth of 10 - 400 kilometers (6 - 250 miles)The upper mantle contains 15.3% of the mantle-crust mass. Fragments have been excavated for our observation by eroded mountain belts and volcanic eruptions. Olivine $(Mg,Fe)_2SiO_4$ and pyroxene $(Mg,Fe)SiO_3$ have been the primary minerals found in this way. These and other minerals are refractory and crystalline at high temperatures; therefore, most settle out of rising magma, either forming new material or never leaving the mantle. Part of the upper mantle called the asthenosphere might be partially molten. (7) Lithosphere Oceanic crust: 0.099% of Earth's mass; depth of 0-10 kilometers (0 - 6 miles) The rigid, outermost layer of the Earth comprising the crust and upper mantle is called the lithosphere. The oceanic crust contains 0.147% of the mantle-crust mass. The majority of the Earth's crust was made through volcanic activity. The oceanic ridge system, a 40,000-kilometer (25,000 mile) network of volcanoes, generates new oceanic crust at the rate of 17 km3 per year, covering the ocean floor with basalt. Hawaii and Iceland are two examples of the accumulation of basalt piles.

The continental crust contains 0.554% of the mantle-crust mass. This is the outer part of the Earth composed essentially of crystalline rocks. These are low-density buoyant minerals dominated mostly by quartz (SiO_2) and feldspars (metal-poor silicates). The crust (both oceanic and continental) is the surface of the Earth; as such, it is the coldest part of our planet. Because cold rocks deform slowly, we refer to this rigid outer shell as the lithosphere (the rocky or strong layer).

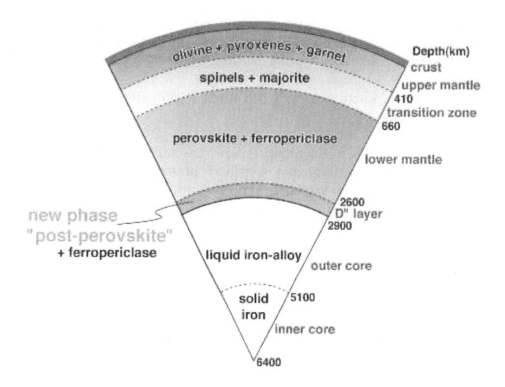

Conclusion

The layers of the earth coincide with the above mentioned hadith of the Prophet. The miracle is in two matters:

(1) The expression of the hadith, 'He will sink down the seven earths on the Day of Resurrection,' indicates the stratification of these "earths" around one center.

(2) The accuracy with which the Prophet of Islam referred to the seven inner layers of earth. The only way for a desert dweller to have known these facts 1400 years ago is through revelation from God.

References Beatty, J. K. and A. Chaikin, eds. The New Solar System. Massachusetts: Sky Publishing, 3rd Edition, 1990.Press, Frank and Raymond Siever. Earth. New York: W. H. Freeman and Company, 1986.Seeds, Michael A. Horizons. Belmont, California: Wadsworth, 1995.El-Najjar, Zaghloul. Treasures In The Sunnah: A Scientific Approach: Cairo, Al-Falah Foundation, 2004.<u>Sunnah & Science</u> **By:** admin

PROVING THE EXISTENCE OF ALLAH (SWT) TO AN ATHEIST

by Dr. Zakir Naik

CONGRATULATING AN ATHEIST

Normally, when I meet an atheist, the first thing I like to do is to congratulate him and say, " My special congratulations to you", because most of the people who believe in God are doing blind belief - he is a Christian, because his father is a Christian; he is a Hindu, because his father is a Hindu; the majority of the people in the world are blindly following the religion of their fathers. An atheist, on the other hand, even though he may belong to a religious family, uses his intellect to deny the existence of God; what ever concept or qualities of God he may have learnt in his religion may not seem to be logical to him.

My Muslim brothers may question me, "Zakir, why are you congratulating an atheist?" The reason that I am congratulating an atheist is because he agrees with the first part of the Shahada i.e. the Islamic Creed, 'La ilaaha' - meaning 'there is no God'.

So half my job is already done; now the only part left is 'il lallah' i.e. 'BUT ALLAH' which I shall do Insha Allah. With others (who are not atheists) I have to first remove from their minds the wrong concept of God they may have and then put the correct concept of one true God.

LOGICAL CONCEPT OF GOD

My first question to the atheist will be: "What is the definition of God?" For a person to say there is no God, he should know what is the meaning of God. If I hold a book and say that 'this is a pen', for the opposite person to say, 'it is not a pen', he should know what is the definition of a pen, even if he does not know nor is able to recognise or identify the object I am holding in my hand. For him to say this is not a pen, he should at least know what a pen means. Similarly for an atheist to say 'there is no God', he should at least know the concept of God. His concept of God would be derived from the surroundings in which he lives. The god that a large number of people worship has got human qualities - therefore he does not believe in such a god. Similarly a Muslim too does not and should not believe in such false gods.

If a non-Muslim believes that Islam is a merciless religion with something to do with terrorism; a religion which does not give rights to women; a religion which contradicts science; in his limited sense that non-Muslim is correct to reject such Islam. The problem is he has a wrong picture of Islam. Even I reject such a false picture of Islam, but at the same time, it becomes my duty as a Muslim to present the correct picture of Islam to that non-Muslim i.e. Islam is a merciful religion, it gives equal rights to the women, it is not incompatible with logic, reason and science; if I present the correct facts about Islam, that non-Muslim may Inshallah accept Islam.

Similarly the atheist rejects the false gods and the duty of every Muslim is to present the correct concept of God which he shall Insha Allah not refuse.

(You may refer to my article, 'Concept of God in Islam', for more details)

QUR'AN AND MODERN SCIENCE

The methods of proving the existence of God with usage of the material provided in the 'Concept of God in Islam' to an atheist may satisfy some but not all. Many atheists demand a scientific proof for the existence of God. I agree that today is the age of science and technology. Let us use scientific knowledge to kill two birds with one stone, i.e. to prove the existence of God and simultaneously prove that the Qur'an is a revelation of God.

If a new object or a machine, which no one in the world has ever seen or heard of before, is shown to an atheist or any person and then a question is asked, " Who is the first person who will be able to provide details of the mechanism of this unknown object? After little bit of thinking, he will reply, 'the creator of that object.' Some may say 'the producer' while others may say 'the manufacturer.' What ever answer the person gives, keep it in your mind, the answer will always be either the creator, the producer, the manufacturer or some what of the same meaning, i.e. the person who has made it or created it. Don't grapple with words, whatever answer he gives, the meaning will be same, therefore accept it.

SCIENTIFIC FACTS MENTIONED IN THE QUR'AN: for details on this subject please refer to my book, 'THE QUR'AN AND MODERN SCIENCE – COMPATIBLE OR INCOMPATIBLE?

THEORY OF PROBABILITY

In mathematics there is a theory known as 'Theory of Probability'. If you have two options, out of which one is right, and one is wrong, the chances that you will chose the right one is half, i.e. one out of the two will be correct. You have 50% chances of being correct. Similarly if you toss a coin the chances that your guess will be correct is 50% (1 out of 2) i.e. 1/2. If you toss a coin the second time, the chances that you will be correct in the second toss is again 50% i.e. half. But the chances that you will be correct in both the tosses is half multiplied by half (1/2 x 1/2) which is equal to 1/4 i.e. 50% of 50% which is equal to 25%. If you toss a coin the third time, chances that you will be correct all three times is (1/2 x 1/2 x 1/2) that is 1/8 or 50% of 50% of 50% that is 12½%.

A dice has got six sides. If you throw a dice and guess any number between 1 to 6, the chances that your guess will be correct is 1/6. If you throw the dice the second time, the chances that your guess will be correct in both the throws is (1/6 x 1/6) which is equal to 1/36. If you throw the dice the third time, the chances that all your three guesses are correct is (1/6 x 1/6 x 1/6) is equal to 1/216 that is less than 0.5 %.

Let us apply this theory of probability to the Qur'an, and assume that a person has guessed all the information that is mentioned in the Qur'an which was unknown at that time. Let us discuss the probability of all the guesses being simultaneously correct.

At the time when the Qur'an was revealed, people thought the world was flat, there are several other options for the shape of the earth. It could be triangular, it could be quadrangular, pentagonal, hexagonal, heptagonal, octagonal, spherical, etc. Lets assume there are about 30 different options for the shape of the earth. The Qur'an rightly says it is spherical, if it was a guess the chances of the guess being correct is 1/30. The light of the moon can be its own light or a reflected light. The Qur'an rightly says it is a reflected light. If it is a guess, the chances that it will be correct is 1/2 and the probability that both the guesses i.e the earth is spherical and the light of the moon is reflected light is 1/30 x 1/2 = 1/60.

Further, the Qur'an also mentions every living thing is made of water. Every living thing can be made up of either wood, stone, copper, aluminum, steel, silver, gold, oxygen, nitrogen, hydrogen, oil, water, cement, concrete, etc. The options are say about 10,000. The Qur'an rightly says that everything is made up of water. If it is a guess, the chances that it will be correct is 1/10,000 and the probability of all the three guesses i.e. the earth is spherical, light of moon is reflected light and everything is created from water being correct is 1/30 x 1/2 x 1/10,000 = 1/60,000 which is equal to about .0017%.

The Qur'an speaks about hundreds of things that were not known to men at the time of its revelation. Only in three options the result is .0017%. I leave it upto you, to work out the probability if all the hundreds of the unknown facts were guesses, the chances of all of them being correct guesses simultaneously and there being not a single wrong guess. It is beyond human capacity to make all correct guesses without a single mistake, which itself is sufficient to prove to a logical person that the origin of the Qur'an is Divine.

CREATOR IS THE AUTHOR OF THE QUR'AN

The only logical answer to the question as to who could have mentioned all these scientific facts 1400 years ago before they were discovered, is exactly the same answer initially given by the atheist or any person, to the question who will be the first person who will be able to tell the mechanism of the unknown object. It is the 'CREATOR', the producer, the Manufacturer of the whole universe and its contents. In the English language He is 'God', or more appropriate in the Arabic language, 'ALLAH'.

QUR'AN IS A BOOK OF SIGNS AND NOT SCIENCE

Let me remind you that the Qur'an is not a book of Science, 'S-C-I-E-N-C-E' but a book of Signs 'S-I-G-N-S' i.e. a book of ayaats. The Qur'an contains more than 6,000 ayaats, i.e. 'signs', out of which more than a thousand speak about Science. I am not trying to prove that the Qur'an is the word of God using scientific knowledge as a yard stick because any yardstick is supposed to be more superior than what is being checked or verified. For us Muslims the Qur'an is the Furqan i.e. criteria to judge right from wrong and the ultimate yardstick which is more superior to scientific knowledge.

But for an educated man who is an atheist, scientific knowledge is the ultimate test which he believes in. We do know that science many a times takes 'U' turns, therefore I have restricted the examples only to

scientific facts which have sufficient proof and evidence and not scientific theories based on assumptions. Using the ultimate yardstick of the atheist, I am trying to prove to him that the Qur'an is the word of God and it contains the scientific knowledge which is his yardstick which was discovered recently, while the Qur'an was revealed 1400 year ago. At the end of the discussion, we both come to the same conclusion that God though superior to science, is not incompatible with it.

SCIENCE IS ELIMINATING MODELS OF GOD BUT NOT GOD

Francis Bacon, the famous philosopher, has rightly said that a little knowledge of science makes man an atheist, but an in-depth study of science makes him a believer in God. Scientists today are eliminating models of God, but they are not eliminating God. If you translate this into Arabic, it is La illaha illal la, There is no god, (god with a small 'g' that is fake god) but God (with a capital 'G').

Surah Fussilat:

"Soon We will show them our signs in the (farthest) regions (of the earth), and in their own souls, until it becomes manifest to them that this is the Truth. Is it not enough that thy Lord doth witness all things?"
[Al-Quran 41:53]

EVOLUTION AN UNPROVEN THEORY : Is there a guarantee that there is 100% evidence of it? no as simple as that.Their stories of evidences Based on bone similarities has no evidence how truthful they are because its mostly based on opinions.Fruits &vegetables have vitamins on them does it mean we came from them?Dogs have calcium in their bones.we have vitamins & calcium in our body ,so does it mean we came from them. God created the entire world matchable,livable,sutable for all humans & creatures.And he made us with similarities.All humans & animals breath from air,drink water.all living things,even trees have water in them like all humans.If god wants to create a cockroach a tree a bird a fish with human blood in them of course he can he is the creater.Its a miracle of god that we have similarities with monkies.It just proves god created the entire world with similarities with us.It does not prove we came from any animal or monkey.

THE QUR'AAN AND MODERN SCIENCE COMPATIBLE OR INCOMPATIBLE?
By Dr. ZAKIR NAIK ISLAMIC RESEARCH FOUNDATION
In the Name of Allah, Most Gracious, Most Merciful
INTRODUCTION

Ever since the dawn of human life on this planet, Man has always sought to understand Nature, his own place in the scheme of Creation and the purpose of Life itself. In this quest for Truth, spanning many centuries and diverse civilizations, organized religion has shaped human life and determined to a large extent, the course of history. While some religions have been based on books, claimed by their adherents to be divinely inspired, others have relied solely on human experience.

Al-Qur'aan, the main source of the Islamic faith, is a book believed by Muslims, to be of completely Divine origin. Muslims also believe that it contains guidance for all mankind. Since the message of the Qur'aan is believed to be for all times, it should be relevant to every age. Does the Qur'aan pass this test? In this booklet, I intend to give an objective analysis of the Muslim belief regarding the Divine origin of the Qur'aan, in the light of established scientific discoveries.

There was a time, in the history of world civilization, when 'miracles', or what was perceived to be a miracle, took precedence over human reason and logic. But how do we define the term 'miracle'? A miracle is anything that takes place out of the normal course of life and for which humankind has no explanation. However, we must be careful before we accept something as a miracle. An article in 'The Times of India' Mumbai, in 1993 reported that 'a saint' by the name 'Baba Pilot' claimed to have stayed continuously submerged under water in a tank for three consecutive days and nights. However, when reporters wanted to examine the base of the tank of water where he claimed to have performed this 'miraculous' feat, he refused to let them do so. He argued by asking as to how one could examine the womb of a mother that gives birth to a child. The 'Baba' was hiding something. It was a gimmick simply to gain publicity. Surely, no modern man with even the slightest inkling towards rational thinking would accept such a 'miracle'. If such false miracles are the tests of divinity, then we would have to accept Mr. P. C. Sorcar, the world famous magician known for his ingenious magical tricks and illusions, as the best God-man.

A book, claiming Divine origin, is in effect, claiming to be a miracle. Such a claim should be easily verifiable in any age, according to the standards of that age. Muslims believe, that the Qur'aan is the last and final revelation of God, the miracle of miracles revealed as a mercy to mankind. Let us therefore investigate the veracity of this belief.

I would like to thank Brother Musaddique Thange for his editorial assistance. May Allah (swt) reward him for his efforts, Aameen

THE CHALLENGE OF THE QUR'AAN

Literature and poetry have been instruments of human expression and creativity, in all cultures. The world also witnessed an age when literature and poetry occupied pride of position, similar to that now enjoyed by science and technology.Muslims as well as non-Muslims agree that Al-Qur'aan is Arabic literature par excellence - that it is the best Arabic literature on the face of the earth. The Qur'aan, challenges mankind in the following verses:

"And if ye are in doubt As to what We have revealed From time to time to Our Servant, then produce a Soorah Like thereunto; And call your witnesses or helpers (If there are any) besides Allah, If your (doubts) are true. But if ye cannot –And of a surety you cannot. hen fear the Fire Whose fuel is Men and Stones – Which is prepared for those Who reject Faith." [Al-Qur'aan 2:23-24] ₁

The same notation is followed throughout the book. References and translation of the Qur'aan are from the translation of the Qur'aan by Abdullah Yusuf Ali, new revised edition, 1989, published by Amana Corporation, Maryland, USA.The challenge of the Qur'aan, is to produce a single *Soorah* (chapter) like the *Soorahs* it contains. The same challenge is repeated in the Qur'aan several times. The challenge to produce a *Soorah*, which, in beauty, eloquence, depth and meaning is at least somewhat similar to a Qur'aanic *Soorah* remains unmet to this day. A modern rational man, however, would never accept a religious scripture, which says, in the best possible poetic language, that the world is flat. This is because we live in an age, where human reason, logic and science are given primacy. Not many would accept the Qur'aan's extraordinarily beautiful language, as proof of its Divine origin. Any scripture

₁ Al-Qur'an 2:23-24 indicates *Soorah* or Chapter No. 2 and *Ayaat* or Verses 23 and 24.

claiming to be a divine revelation must also be acceptable on the strength of its own reason and logic.

According to the famous physicist and Nobel Prize winner, Albert Einstein, "Science without religion is lame. Religion without science is blind." Let us therefore study the Qur'aan, and analyze whether **The Qur'aan and Modern Science are compatible or incompatible?**

The Qur'aan is not a book of science but a book of 'signs', i.e. *ayat*s. There are more than six thousand 'signs' in the Qur'aan of which more than a thousand deal with science. We all know that many a times Science takes a 'U-turn'. In this book I have considered only established scientific facts and not mere hypotheses and theories that are based on assumptions and are not backed by proof.

I. ASTRONOMY

CREATION OF THE UNIVERSE: 'THE BIG BANG'

The creation of the universe is explained by astrophysicists in a widely accepted phenomenon, popularly known as the 'Big Bang'. It is supported by observational and experimental data gathered by astronomers and astrophysicists for decades. According to the 'Big Bang', the whole universe was initially one big mass (Primary Nebula). Then there was a 'Big Bang' (Secondary Separation) which resulted in the formation of Galaxies. These then divided to form stars, planets, the sun, the moon, etc. The origin of the universe was unique and the probability of it occurring by 'chance' is zero. The Qur'aan contains the following verse, regarding the origin of the universe: **"Do not the Unbelievers see That the heavens and the earth Were joined together (as one Unit of Creation), before We clove them asunder?"** [Al-Qur'aan 21:30]

The striking congruence between the Qur'aanic verse and the 'Big Bang' is inescapable! How could a book, which first appeared in the deserts of Arabia 1400 years ago, contain this profound scientific truth?

THERE WAS AN INITIAL GASEOUS MASS BEFORE THE CREATION OF GALAXIES

Scientists say that before the galaxies in the universe were formed, celestial matter was initially in the form of gaseous matter. In short, huge gaseous matter or clouds were present before the formation of the galaxies. To describe initial celestial matter, the word 'smoke' is more appropriate than gas. The following Qur'aanic verse refers to this state of the universe by the word *dhukhan* which means smoke.

"Moreover, He Comprehended In His design the sky, And it had been (as) smoke: He said to it And to the earth: 'Come ye together, Willingly or unwillingly.' They said: 'We do come (Together), in willing obedience.'" [Al-Qur'aan 41:11]

Again, this fact is a corollary to the 'Big Bang' and was not known to the Arabs during the time of Prophet Muhammad (pbuh). What then, could have been the source of this knowledge?

THE SPHERICAL SHAPE OF THE EARTH

In early times, people believed that the earth is flat. For centuries, men were afraid to venture out too far, lest they should fall off the edge. Sir Francis Drake was the first person who proved that the earth is spherical when he sailed around it in 1597. Consider the following Qur'aanic verse regarding the alternation of day and night: **"Seest thou not that Allah merges Night into Day And He merges Day into Night?"** [Al-Qur'aan 31:29]

Merging here means that the night slowly and gradually changes to day and vice versa. This phenomenon can only take place if the earth is spherical. If the earth was flat, there would have been a sudden change from night to day and from day to night.

The following verse also alludes to the spherical shape of the earth: **"He created the heavens And the earth In true (proportions): He makes the Night Overlap the Day, and the Day Overlap the Night."** [Al-Qur'aan 39:5]

The Arabic word used here is *Kawwara* meaning 'to overlap' or 'to coil'– the way a turban is wound around the head. The overlapping or coiling of the day and night can only take place if the earth is spherical.

The earth is not exactly round like a ball, but geo-spherical i.e. it is flattened at the poles. The following verse contains a description of the earth's shape:

"**And the earth, moreover, Hath He made egg shaped.**" [2] [Al-Qur'aan 79:30]

The Arabic word for egg here is *dahaha*, which means an ostrich-egg. The shape of an ostrich-egg resembles the geo-spherical shape of the earth. Thus the Qur'aan correctly describes the shape of the earth, though the prevalent notion when the Qur'aan was revealed was that the earth is flat.

THE LIGHT OF THE MOON IS REFLECTED LIGHT

It was believed by earlier civilizations that the moon emanates its own light. Science now tells us that the light of the moon is reflected light. However this fact was mentioned in the Qur'aan 1,400 years ago in the following verse:.

"**Blessed is He Who made Constellations in the skies, And placed therein a Lamp And a Moon giving light.**" [Al-Qur'aan 25:61]

The Arabic word for the sun in the Qur'aan, is *shams*. It is referred to as *siraaj*, which means a 'torch' or as *wahhaaj* which means 'a blazing lamp' or as *diya* which means 'shining glory'. All three descriptions are appropriate to the sun, since it generates intense heat and light by its internal combustion. The Arabic word for the moon is *qamar* and it is described in the Qur'aan as *muneer*, which is a body that gives *nur* i.e. light. Again, the Qur'aanic description matches perfectly with the true nature of the moon, which does not give off light itself and is an inert body that reflects the light of the sun. Not once in the Qur'aan, is the moon mentioned as *siraaj*, *wahhaaj* or *diya* or the sun as *nur* or *muneer*. This implies that the Qur'aan recognizes the difference between the nature of sunlight and moonlight.

[2] The Arabic word *dahaha* has been translated by A. Yusuf Ali as "vast expanse", which also is correct. The word *dahaha* also means an ostrich-egg.

Consider the following verses related to the nature of light from the sun and the moon: "**It is He who made the sun To be a shining glory And the moon to be a light (Of beauty).**" [Al-Qur'aan 10:5]

"**See ye not How Allah has created The seven heavens One above another, "And made the moon A light in their midst, and made the sun As a (Glorious) Lamp?**" [Al-Qur'aan 71:15-16]

THE SUN ROTATES

For a long time European philosophers and scientists believed that the earth stood still in the centre of the universe and every other body including the sun moved around it. In the West, this geocentric concept of the universe was prevalent right from the time of Ptolemy in the second century B.C. In 1512, Nicholas Copernicus put forward his Heliocentric Theory of Planetary Motion, which asserted that the sun is motionless at the centre of the solar system with the planets revolving around it.

In 1609, the German scientist Yohannus Keppler published the *'Astronomia Nova'*. In this he concluded that not only do the planets move in elliptical orbits around the sun, they also rotate upon their axes at irregular speeds. With this knowledge it became possible for European scientists to explain correctly many of the mechanisms of the solar system including the sequence of night and day.

After these discoveries, it was thought that the Sun was stationary and did not rotate about its axis like the Earth. I remember having studied this fallacy from Geography books during my school days. Consider the following Qur'aanic verse: **"It is He Who created The Night and the Day, And the sun and the moon: All (the celestial bodies) Swim along, each in its Rounded course."** [Al-Qur'aan 21:33]

The Arabic word used in the above verse is *yasbahûn* . The word *yasbahûn* is derived from the word *sabah*a. It carries with it the idea of motion that comes from any moving body. If you use the word for a man on the ground, it would not mean that he is rolling but would mean he is walking or running. If you use the word for a man in water it would not mean that he is floating but would mean that he is swimming.

Similarly, if you use the word *yasbah* for a celestial body such as the sun it would not mean that it is only flying through space but would mean that it is also rotating as it goes through space. Most of the school textbooks have incorporated the fact that the sun rotates about its axis. The rotation of the sun about its own axis can be proved with the help of an equipment that projects the image of the sun on the table top so that one can examine the image of the sun without being blinded. It is noticed that the sun has spots which complete a circular motion once every 25 days i.e. the sun takes approximately 25 days to rotate around its axis.

In fact, the sun travels through space at roughly 150 miles per second, and takes about 200 million years to complete one revolution around the center of our Milky Way Galaxy.

"It is not permitted To the Sun to catch up The Moon, nor can The Night outstrip the Day: Each (just) swims along In (its own) orbit (According to Law)." [Al-Qur'aan 36:40]

This verse mentions an essential fact discovered by modern astronomy, i.e. the existence of the individual orbits of the Sun and the Moon, and their journey through space with their own motion. The 'fixed place' towards, which the sun travels, carrying with it the solar system, has been located exactly by modern astronomy. It has been given a name, the Solar Apex. The solar system is indeed moving in space towards a point situated in the constellation of Hercules (alpha Layer) whose exact location is firmly established.

The moon rotates around its axis in the same duration that it takes to revolve around the earth. It takes approximately 29½ days to complete one rotation. One cannot help but be amazed at the scientific accuracy of the Qur'aanic verses. Should we not ponder over the question: "What was the source of knowledge contained in the Qur'aan?"

THE SUN WILL EXTINGUISH AFTER A CERTAIN PERIOD

The light of the sun is due to a chemical process on its surface that has been taking place continuously for the past five billion years. It will come to an end at some point of time in the future when the sun will be totally extinguished leading to extinction of all life on earth. Regarding the impermanence of the sun's existence the Qur'aan says: **"And the Sun Runs its course For a** period determined For it; that is The decree of (Him) The exalted in Might, The All-Knowing." [Al-Qur'aan 36:38] [3]

The Arabic word used here is *mustaqar*r, which means a place or time that is determined. Thus the Qur'aan says that the sun runs towards a determined place, and will do so only up to a pre-determined period of time – meaning that it will end or extinguish.

THE PRESENCE OF INTERSTELLAR MATTER

Space outside organized astronomical systems was earlier assumed to be a vacuum . Astrophysicists later discovered the presence of bridges of matter in this interstellar space. These bridges of matter are called plasma, and consist of completely ionized gas containing equal number of free electrons and positive ions. Plasma is sometimes called the fourth state of matter (besides the three known states viz. solid, liquid and gas). The Qur'aan mentions the presence of this interstellar material in the following verse: **"He Who created the heavens And the earth and all That is between."** [Al-Qur'aan 25:59]

It would be ridiculous, for anybody to even suggest that the presence of interstellar galactic material was known 1400 years ago.

[3] A similar message is conveyed in the Qur'an in 13:2, 35:13, 39:5 and 39:21.
The Qur'aan and Modern Science: Compatible or Incompatible?

THE EXPANDING UNIVERSE

In 1925, an American astronomer by the name of Edwin Hubble, provided observational evidence that all galaxies are receding from one another, which implies that the universe is expanding. The expansion of the universe is now an established scientific fact. This is what Al-Qur'aan says regarding the nature of the universe: **"With the power and skill Did We construct The Firmament: For it is We Who create The vastness of Space."** [Al-Qur'aan 51:47]

The Arabic word *mûsi'ûn* is correctly translated as 'expanding it', and it refers to the creation of the expanding vastness of the universe. Stephen Hawking, in his book, 'A Brief History of Time', says, "The discovery that the universe is expanding was one of the great intellectual revolutions of the 20th century."

The Qur'aan mentioned the expansion of the universe, before man even learnt to build a telescope! Some may say that the presence of astronomical facts in the Qur'aan is not surprising since the Arabs were advanced in the field of astronomy. They are correct in acknowledging the advancement of the Arabs in the field of astronomy. However they fail to realize that the Qur'aan was revealed centuries before the Arabs excelled in astronomy. Moreover many of the scientific facts mentioned above regarding astronomy, such as the origin of the universe with a Big Bang, were not known to the Arabs even at the peak of their scientific advancement. The scientific facts mentioned in the Qur'aan are therefore not due to the Arabs' advancement in astronomy. Indeed, the reverse is true. The Arabs advanced in astronomy, because astronomy occupies a place in the Qur'aan.

II. PHYSICS
THE EXISTENCE OF SUBATOMIC PARTICLES

In ancient times a well-known theory by the name of 'Theory of Atomism' was widely accepted. This theory was originally proposed by the Greeks, in particular by a man called Democritus, who lived about 23 centuries ago. Democritus and the people that came after him, assumed that the smallest unit of matter was the atom. The Arabs used to believe the same. The Arabic word *dharrah* most commonly meant an atom. In recent times modern science has discovered that it is possible to split even an atom. That the atom can be split further is a development of the 20th century. Fourteen centuries ago this concept would have appeared unusual even to an Arab. For him the *dharrah* was the limit beyond which one could not go. The following Qur'aanic verse however, refuses to acknowledge this limit: **"The Unbelievers say, 'Never to us will come The Hour': say, 'Nay! But most surely, By my Lord, it will come Upon you – by Him Who knows the unseen – From Whom is not hidden The least little atom In the Heavens or on earth: Nor is there anything less Than that, or greater, but Is in the Record Perspicuous.'"** [Al-Qur'aan 34:3] [4]

This verse refers to the Omniscience of God, His knowledge of all things, hidden or apparent. It then goes further and says that God is aware of everything, including what is smaller or bigger than the atom. Thus the verse clearly shows that it is possible for something smaller than the atom to exist, a fact discovered only recently by modern science.

[4] A similar message is conveyed in the Qur'an in 10:61.
The Qur'aan and Modern Science: Compatible or Incompatible?

III. GEOGRAPHY
THE WATER CYCLE

In 1580, Bernard Palissy was the first man to describe the present day concept of 'water cycle'. He described how water evaporates from the oceans and cools to form clouds. The clouds move inland where they rise, condense and fall as rain. This water gathers as lakes and streams and flows back to the ocean in a continuous cycle. In the 7th century B.C., Thales of Miletus believed that surface spray of the oceans was picked up by the wind and carried inland to fall as rain. In earlier times people did not know the source of underground water. They thought the water of the oceans, under the effect of winds, was thrust towards the interior of the continents. They also believed that the water returned by a secret passage, or the Great Abyss. This passage is connected to the oceans and has been called the 'Tartarus', since Plato's time. Even Descartes, a great thinker of the eighteenth century, subscribed to this view. Till the nineteenth century, Aristotle's theory was prevalent. According to this theory, water was condensed in cool mountain caverns and formed underground lakes that fed springs. Today, we know that the rainwater that seeps into the cracks of the ground is responsible for this.

The water cycle is described by the Qur'aan in the following verses: **"Seest thou not that Allah Sends down rain from The sky, and leads it Through springs in the earth? Then He causes to grow, Therewith, produce of various Colours."** [Al-Qur'aan 39:21]

"He sends down rain From the sky And with it gives life to The earth after it is dead: Verily in that are Signs For those who are wise." [Al-Qur'aan 30:24]

"And We send down water From the sky according to (Due) measure, and We cause it To soak in the soil; And We certainly are able To drain it off (with ease)." [Al-Qur'aan 23:18]

No other text dating back 1400 years ago gives such an accurate description of the water cycle.

WINDS IMPREGNATE THE CLOUDS

"**And We send the fecundating winds, Then cause the rain to descend From the sky, therewith providing You with water (in abundance).**" [Al-Qur'aan 15:22]

The Arabic word used here is *lawâqih,* which is the plural of *laqih* from *laqah*a, which means to impregnate or fecundate. In this context, impregnate means that the wind pushes the clouds together increasing the condensation that causes lightning and thus rain. A similar description is found in the Qur'aan: "**It is Allah Who sends The Winds, and they raise The Clouds: then does He Spread them in the sky As He wills, and break them Into fragments, until thou seest Raindrops issue from the midst Thereof: then when He has Made them reach such Of His servants as He wills, Behold, they do rejoice!**" [Al-Qur'aan 30:48]

The Qur'aanic descriptions are absolutely accurate and agree perfectly with modern data on hydrology. The water cycle is described in several verses of the Glorious Qur'aan, including 3:9, 7:57, 13:17, 25:48- 49, 36:34, 50:9-11, 56:68-70, 67:30 and 86:11.

IV. GEOLOGY

MOUNTAINS ARE LIKE PEGS (STAKES)

In Geology, the phenomenon of 'folding' is a recently discovered fact. Folding is responsible for the formation of mountain ranges. The earth's crust, on which we live, is like a solid shell, while the deeper layers are hot and fluid, and thus inhospitable to any form of life. It is also known that the stability of the mountains is linked to the phenomenon of folding, for it was the folds that were to provide foundations for the reliefs that constitute the mountains. Geologists tell us that the radius of the Earth is about 3,750 miles and the crust on which we live is very thin, ranging between 1 to 30 miles. Since the crust is thin, it has a high possibility of shaking. Mountains act like stakes or tent pegs that hold the earth's crust and give it stability. The Qur'aan contains exactly such a description in the following verse: "**Have We not made The earth as a wide Expanse, And the mountains as pegs?**" [Al-Qur'aan 78:6-7]

The word *awtad* means stakes or pegs (like those used to anchor a tent); they are the deep foundations of geological folds. A book named 'Earth' is considered as a basic reference textbook on geology in many universities around the world. One of the authors of this book is Frank Press, who was the President of the Academy of Sciences in the USA for 12 years and was the Science Advisor to former US President Jimmy Carter. In this book he illustrates the mountain in a wedge-shape and the mountain itself as a small part of the whole, whose root is deeply entrenched in the ground.[5] According to Dr. Press, the mountains play an important role in stabilizing the crust of the earth.

The Qur'aan clearly mentions the function of the mountains in preventing the earth from shaking: **"And We have set on the earth Mountains standing firm, Lest it should shake with them."** [Al-Qur'aan 21:31]

[5] *Earth*, Press and Siever, p. 435. Also see *Earth Science*, Tarbuck and Lutgens, p. 157.

The Qur'aanic descriptions are in perfect agreement with modern geological data.

MOUNTAINS FIRMLY FIXED

The surface of the earth is broken into many rigid plates that are about 100 km in thickness. These plates float on a partially molten region called aesthenosphere. Mountain formations occur at the boundary of the plates. The earth's crust is 5 km thick below oceans, about 35 km thick below flat continental surfaces and almost 80 km thick below great mountain ranges. These are the strong foundations on which mountains stand. The Qur'aan also speaks about the strong mountain foundations in the following verse: **"And the mountains Hath He firmly fixed."** [Al-Qur'aan 79:32] [6]

[6] A similar message is contained in the Qur'an in 88:19, 31:10 and 16:15

V. OCEANOLOGY

BARRIER BETWEEN SWEET AND SALT WATERS

Consider the following Qur'aanic verses: **"He has let free the two bodies Of flowing water, Meeting together: Between them is a Barrier Which they do not transgress."** [Al-Qur'aan 55:19-20]

In the Arabic text the word *barzakh* means a barrier or a partition. This barrier is not a physical partition. The Arabic word *maraja* literally means 'they both meet and mix with each other'. Early commentators of the Qur'aan were unable to explain the two opposite meanings for the two bodies of water, i.e. they meet and mix, and at the same time, there is a barrier between them. Modern Science has discovered that in the places where two different seas meet, there is a barrier between them. This barrier divides the two seas so that each sea has its own temperature, salinity and density. [7] Oceanologists are now in a better position to explain this verse. There is slanted unseen water barrier between the two seas through which water from one sea passes to the other. But when the water from one sea enters the other sea, it loses its distinctive characteristic and becomes homogenized with the other water. In a way this barrier serves as a transitional homogenizing area for the two waters. This scientific phenomenon mentioned in the Qur'aan was also confirmed by Dr. William Hay who is a well-known marine scientist and Professor of Geological Sciences at the University of Colorado, U.S.A. The Qur'aan mentions this phenomenon also in the following verse: **"And made a separating bar between the two bodies Of flowing water?"** [Al-Qur'aan 27:61]

This phenomenon occurs in several places, including the divider between the Mediterranean and the Atlantic Ocean at Gibralter. But when the Qur'aan speaks about the divider between fresh and salt water, it mentions the

[7] *Principles of Oceanography*, Davis, pp. 92-93.

existence of "a forbidding partition" with the barrier. **"It is He Who has Let free the two bodies Of flowing water: One palatable and sweet, And the other salty and bitter; Yet has He Made a barrier between them, And a partition that is forbidden To be passed."** [Al-Qur'aan 25:53]

Modern science has discovered that in estuaries, where fresh (sweet) and saltwater meet, the situation is somewhat different from that found in places where two seas meet. It has been discovered that what distinguishes fresh water from salt water in estuaries is a "pycnocline zone with a marked density discontinuity separating the two layers." [8] This partition (zone of separation) has salinity different from both the fresh water and the salt water. [9] This phenomenon occurs in several places, including Egypt, where the river Nile flows into the Mediterranean Sea.

DARKNESS IN THE DEPTHS OF THE OCEAN

Prof. Durga Rao is an expert in the field of Marine Geology and was a professor at King Abdul Aziz University in Jeddah. He was asked to comment on the following verse: **"Or (the Unbelievers' state) Is like the depths of darkness In a vast deep ocean, Overwhelmed with billow Topped by billow, Topped by (dark) clouds: Depths of darkness, one Above another: if a man Stretches out his hand, He can hardly see it! For any to whom Allah Giveth not light, there is no light!"** [Al-Qur'aan 24:40]

Prof. Rao said that scientists have only now been able to confirm, with the help of modern equipment that there is darkness in the depths of the ocean. Humans are unable to dive unaided underwater for more than 20 to 30 meters, and cannot survive in the deep oceanic regions at a depth of more than 200 meters. This verse does not refer to all seas because not every sea can be

[8] *Oceanography,* Gross, p. 242. Also see *Introductory Oceanography,* Thurman, pp. 300-301.

[9] *Oceanography,* Gross, p. 244 and *Introductory Oceanography,* Thurman, pp. 300-301.

described as having accumulated darkness layered one over another. It refers especially to a deep sea or deep ocean, as the Qur'aan says, "darkness in a vast deep ocean". This layered darkness in a deep ocean is the result of two causes: A light ray is composed of seven colours. These seven colours are Violet, Indigo, Blue, Green, Yellow, Orange and Red (VIBGYOR). The light ray undergoes refraction when it hits water. The upper 10 to 15 metres of water absorb the red colour. Therefore if a diver is 25 metres under water and gets wounded, he would not be able to see the red colour of his blood, because the red colour does not reach this depth. Similarly orange rays are absorbed at 30 to 50 metres, yellow at 50 to 100 metres, green at 100 to 200 metres, and finally, blue beyond 200 metres and violet and indigo above 200 metres. Due to successive disappearance of colour, one layer after another, the ocean progressively becomes darker, i.e. darkness takes place in layers of light. Below a depth of 1000 meters there is complete darkness. [10]

. The sun's rays are absorbed by clouds, which in turn scatter light rays thus causing a layer of darkness under the clouds. This is the first layer of darkness. When light rays reach the surface of the ocean they are reflected by the wave surface giving it a shiny appearance. Therefore it is the waves which reflect light and cause darkness. The unreflected light penetrates into the depths of the ocean. Therefore the ocean has two parts. The surface characterized by light and warmth and the depth characterized by darkness. The surface is further separated from the deep part of the ocean by waves. The internal waves cover the deep waters of seas and oceans because the deep waters have a higher density than the waters above them. The darkness begins below the internal waves. Even the fish in the depths of the ocean cannot see; their only source of light is from their own bodies.

The Qur'aan rightly mentions: **"Darkness in a vast deep ocean overwhelmed with waves topped by waves"**.

10 *Oceans,* Elder and Pernetta, p. 27.

In other words, above these waves there are more types of waves, i.e. those found on the surface of the ocean. The Qur'aanic verse continues, "topped by (dark) clouds; depths of darkness, one above another."

These clouds as explained are barriers one over the other that further cause darkness by absorption of colours at different levels.

Prof. Durga Rao concluded by saying, "1400 years ago a normal human being could not explain this phenomenon in so much detail. Thus the information must have come from a supernatural source".

VI. BIOLOGY

EVERY LIVING THING IS MADE OF WATER

Consider the following Qur'aanic verse: **"Do not the Unbelievers see that the heavens and the earth were joined together (as one Unit of Creation), before We clove them asunder? We made from water every living thing. Will they not then believe?"** [Al-Qur'aan 21:30]

Only after advances have been made in science, do we now know that cytoplasm, the basic substance of the cell is made up of 80% water. Modern research has also revealed that most organisms consist of 50% to 90% water and that every living entity requires water for its existence. Was it possible 14 centuries ago for any human-being to guess that every living being was made of water? Moreover would such a guess be conceivable by a human being in the deserts of Arabia where there has always been scarcity of water? The following verse refers to the creation of animals from water: **"And Allah has created Every animal from water."** [Al-Qur'aan 24:45]

The following verse refers to the creation of human beings from water: **"It is He Who has Created man from water: Then has He established Relationships of lineage And marriage: for thy Lord Has power (over all things)."** [Al-Qur'aan 25:54]

VII. BOTANY

PLANTS CREATED IN PAIRS, MALE AND FEMALE

Previously humans did not know that plants too have male and female gender distinctions. Botany states that every plant has a male and female gender. Even the plants that are unisexual have distinct elements of both male and female. **"'And has sent Down water from the sky.' With it have We produced Diverse pairs of plants Each separate from the others."** [Al-Qur'aan 20:53]

FRUITS CREATED IN PAIRS, MALE AND FEMALE

"**And fruit Of every kind He made In pairs, two and two.**" [Al-Qur'aan 13:3]

Fruit is the end product of reproduction of the superior plants. The stage preceding fruit is the flower, which has male and female organs (stamens and ovules). Once pollen has been carried to the flower, they bear fruit, which in turn matures and frees its seed. All fruits therefore imply the existence of male and female organs; a fact that is mentioned in the Qur'aan.

In certain species, fruit can come from non-fertilized flowers (parthenocarpic fruit) e.g. bananas, certain types of pineapple, fig, orange, vine, etc. They also have definite sexual characteristics.

EVERYTHING MADE IN PAIRS

"**And of everything We have created pairs.**" [Al-Qur'aan 51:49]

This refers to things other than humans, animals, plants and fruits. It may also be referring to a phenomenon like electricity in which the atoms consist of negatively – and positively – charged electrons and protons.

"**Glory to Allah, Who created In pairs all things that The earth produces, as well as Their own (human) kind And (other) things of which They have no knowledge.**" [Al-Qur'aan 36:36]

The Qur'aan here says that everything is created in pairs, including things that the humans do not know at present and may discover later.

VIII. ZOOLOGY

ANIMALS AND BIRDS LIVE IN COMMUNITIES

"**There is not an animal (That lives) on the earth, Nor a being that flies On its wings, but (forms Part of) communities like you.**" [Al-Qur'aan 6:38]

Research has shown that animals and birds live in communities, i.e. they organize, and live and work together.

THE FLIGHT OF BIRDS

Regarding the flight of birds the Qur'aan says: "**Do they not look at The birds, held poised In the midst of (the air And) the sky? Nothing Holds them up but (the power Of) Allah. Verily in this Are Signs for those who believe.**" [Al-Qur'aan 16:79] A similar message is repeated in the Qur'aan in the verse: "**Do they not observe The birds above them, Spreading their wings And folding them in? None can uphold them Except (Allah) Most Gracious: Truly it is He That watches over all things.**" [Al-Qur'aan 67:19]

The Arabic word *amsaka* literally means, 'to put one's hand on, seize, hold, hold someone back,' which expresses the idea that Allah holds the bird up in His power. These verses stress the extremely close dependence of the birds' behaviour on Divine order. Modern scientific data has shown the degree of perfection attained by certain species of birds with regard to the programming of their movements. It is only the existence of a migratory programme in the genetic code of the birds that can explain the long and complicated journey that very young birds, without any prior experience and without any guide, are able to accomplish. They are also able to return to the departure point on a definite date.

Prof. Hamburger in his book 'Power and Fragility' gives the example of 'mutton-bird' that lives in the Pacific with its journey of over 15,000 miles in the shape of figure '8'. It makes this journey over a period of 6 months and comes back to its departure point with a maximum delay of one week. The highly complicated instructions for such a journey have to be contained in the birds' nervous cells. They are definitely programmed. Should we not reflect on the identity of this 'Programmer'?

THE BEE

"And thy Lord taught the Bee To build its cells in hills, On trees, and in (men's) habitations; Then to eat of all The produce (of the earth), And find with skill the spacious Paths of its Lord." [Al-Qur'aan 16:68-69]

Von-Frisch received the Nobel Prize in 1973 for his research on the behaviour and communication of the bees. The bee, after discovering any new garden or flower, goes back and tells its fellow bees the exact direction and map to get there, which is known as 'bee dance'. The meanings of this insect's movements that are intended to transmit information between worker bees have been discovered scientifically using photography and other methods. The Qur'aan mentions in the above verse how the bee finds with skill the spacious paths of its Lord.

The worker bee or the soldier bee is a female bee. In Soorah Al-Nahl chapter no. 16, verses 68 and 69 the gender used for the bee is the female gender (*fa'slukî* and *kulî*), indicating that the bee that leaves its home for gathering food is a female bee. In other words the soldier or worker bee is a female bee. In fact, in Shakespeare's play, "Henry the Fourth", some of the characters speak about bees and mention that the bees are soldiers and that they have a king. That is what people thought in Shakespearean times. They thought that the worker bees are male bees and they go home and are answerable to a king bee. This, however, is not true. The worker bees are females and they do not report to a king bee but to a queen bee. But it took modern investigations in the last 300 years to discover this.

SPIDER'S WEB / HOME IS FRAGILE

The Qur'aan mentions in Soorah Al-'Ankabût, **"The parable of those who Take protectors other than Allah Is that of the Spider, Who builds (to itself) A house; but truly The flimsiest of houses Is the Spider's house – If they but knew."** [Al-Qur'aan 29:41]

Besides giving the physical description of the spider's web as being very flimsy, delicate and weak, the Qur'aan also stresses on the flimsiness of the relationship in the spider's house, where the female spider many a times kills its mate, the male spider.

LIFESTYLE AND COMMUNICATION OF ANTS

Consider the following Qur'aanic verse: **"And before Solomon were marshaled His hosts – of Jinns and men And birds, and they were all**

Kept in order and ranks. "At length, when they came To a (lowly) valley of ants, One of the ants said: 'O ye ants, get into Your habitations, lest Solomon And his hosts crush you (Under foot) without knowing it.'" [Al-Qur'aan 27:17-18]

In the past, some people would have probably mocked at the Qur'aan, taking it to be a fairy tale book in which ants talk to each other and communicate sophisticated messages. In recent times, research has shown us several facts about the lifestyle of ants, which were not known earlier to humankind. Research has shown that the animals or insects whose lifestyle is closest in resemblance to the lifestyle of human beings are the ants. This can be seen from the following findings regarding ants:

(a) The ants bury their dead in a manner similar to the humans.
(b) They have a sophisticated system of division of labour, whereby they have managers, supervisors, foremen, workers, etc.
(c) Once in a while they meet among themselves to have a 'chat'.
(d) They have an advanced method of communication among themselves.

(e) They hold regular markets wherein they exchange goods.
(f) They store grains for long periods in winter and if the grain begins to bud, they cut the roots, as if they understand that if they leave it to grow, it will rot. If the grains stored by them get wet due to rains, they take these grains out into the sunlight to dry, and once these are dry, they take them back inside as though they know that humidity will cause development of root systems and thereafter rotting of the grain.

IX. MEDICINE
HONEY HAS HEALING PROPERTIES

The bee assimilates juices of various kinds of flowers and fruit and forms within its body the honey, which it stores in its cells of wax. Only a couple of centuries ago man came to know that honey comes from the belly of the bee. This fact was mentioned in the Qur'aan 1,400 years ago in the following verse: **"There issues From within their bodies A drink of varying colours, Wherein is healing for men."** [Al-Qur'aan 16:69]

We are now aware that honey has a healing property and also a mild antiseptic property. The Russians used honey to cover their wounds in World War II. The wound would retain moisture and would leave very little scar tissue. Due to the density of honey, no fungus or bacteria would grow in the wound. A person suffering from an allergy of a particular plant may be given honey from that plant so that the person develops resistance to that allergy. Honey is rich in fructose and vitamin K. Thus the knowledge contained in the Qur'aan regarding honey, its origin and properties, was far ahead of the time it was revealed.

X. PHYSIOLOGY

BLOOD CIRCULATION AND THE PRODUCTION OF MILK

The Qur'aan was revealed 600 years before the Muslim scientist Ibn Nafees described the circulation of the blood and 1,000 years before William Harwey brought this understanding to the Western world. Roughly thirteen centuries before it was known what happens in the intestines to ensure that organs are nourished by the process of digestive absorption, a verse in the Qur'aan described the source of the constituents of milk, in conformity with these notions. To understand the Qur'aanic verse concerning the above concepts, it is important to know that chemical reactions occur in the intestines and that, from there, substances extracted from food pass into the blood stream via a complex system; sometimes by way of the liver, depending on their chemical nature. The blood transports them to all the organs of the body, among which are the milk-producing mammary glands.

In simple terms, certain substances from the contents of the intestines enter into the vessels of the intestinal wall itself, and these substances are transported by the blood stream to the various organs.

This concept must be fully appreciated if we wish to understand the following verse in the Qur'aan: **"And verily in cattle there is A lesson for you. We give you to drink Of what is inside their bodies, Coming from a conjunction Between the contents of the Intestine and the blood, A milk pure and pleasant for Those who drink it."** [Al-Qur'aan 16:66] 11

"And in cattle (too) ye Have an instructive example: From within their bodies We produce (milk) for you To drink; there are, in them, (Besides),

11 Translation of this Qur'anic verse is from the book "The Bible, the Qur'an and Science" by Dr. Maurice Bucaille.

numerous (other) Benefits for you; And of their (meat) ye eat." [Al-Qur'aan 23:21]

The Qur'aanic description of the production of milk in cattle is strikingly similar to what modern physiology has discovered.

XI. EMBRYOLOGY

MAN IS CREATED FROM *ALAQ*
A LEECH-LIKE SUBSTANCE

A few years ago a group of Arabs collected all information concerning embryology from the Qur'aan, and followed the instruction of the Qur'aan: **"If ye realise this not, ask Of those who possess the Message."** [Al-Qur'aan 16:43 & 21:7]

All the information from the Qur'aan so gathered, was translated into English and presented to Prof. (Dr.) Keith Moore, who was the Professor of Embryology and Chairman of the Department of Anatomy at the University of Toronto, in Canada. At present he is one of the highest authorities in the field of Embryology. He was asked to give his opinion regarding the information present in the Qur'aan concerning the field of embryology. After carefully examining the translation of the Qur'aanic verses presented to him,

Dr. Moore said that most of the information concerning embryology mentioned in the Qur'aan is in perfect conformity with modern discoveries in the field of embryology and does not conflict with them in any way. He added that there were however a few verses, on whose scientific accuracy he could not comment. He could not say whether the statements were true or false, since he himself was not aware of the information contained therein. There was also no mention of this information in modern writings and studies on embryology. One such verse is: **"Proclaim! (or Read!) In the name Of thy Lord and Cherisher, Who created – Created man, out of A (mere) clot Of congealed blood."** [Al-Qur'aan 96:1-2]

The word *alaq* besides meaning a congealed clot of blood also means something that clings, a leech-like substance. Dr. Keith Moore had no knowledge whether an embryo in the initial stages appears like a leech. To check this out he studied the initial stage of the embryo under a very powerful microscope in his laboratory and compared what he observed with a diagram of a leech and he was astonished at the striking resemblance between the two!

In the same manner, he acquired more information on embryology that was hitherto not known to him, from the Qur'aan. Dr. Keith Moore answered about eighty questions dealing with embryological data mentioned in the Qur'aan and Hadith. Noting that the information contained in the Qur'aan and Hadith was in full agreement with the latest discoveries in the field of embryology, Prof. Moore said, "If I was asked these questions thirty years ago, I would not have been able to answer half of them for lack of scientific information"

Dr. Keith Moore had earlier authored the book, 'The Developing Human'. After acquiring new knowledge from the Qur'aan, he wrote, in 1982, the 3rd edition of the same book, 'The Developing Human'. The book was the recipient of an award for the best medical book written by a single author. This book has been translated into several major languages of the world and is used as a textbook of embryology in the first year of medical studies.

In 1981, during the Seventh Medical Conference in Dammam, Saudi Arabia, Dr. Moore said, "It has been a great pleasure for me to help clarify statements in the Qur'aan about human development. It is clear to me that these statements must have come to Muhammad from God or Allah, because almost all of this knowledge was not discovered until many centuries later. This proves to me that Muhammad must have been a messenger of God or Allah." [12]

Dr. Joe Leigh Simpson, Chairman of the Department of Obstetrics and Gynaecology, at the Baylor College of Medicine, Houston, U.S.A., proclaims: "...these Hadiths, sayings of Muhammad (pbuh) could not have been obtained on the basis of the scientific knowledge that was available at the time of the writer (7th century). It follows that not only is there no conflict between genetics and religion (Islam) but in fact religion (Islam) may guide science by adding revelation to some of the traditional scientific approaches... there exist statements in the Qur'aan shown centuries later to

[12] The reference for this statment is the video tape titled *'This is the Truth'*. For a

MAN CREATED FROM A DROP EMITTED FROM BETWEEN THE BACK BONE AND THE RIBS

"Now let man but think From what he is created! He is created from A drop emitted – Proceeding from between The back bone and the ribs." [Al-Qur'aan 86:5-7]

In embryonic stages, the reproductive organs of the male and female, i.e. the testicles and the ovaries, begin their development near the kidney between the spinal column and the eleventh and twelfth ribs. Later they descend; the female gonads (ovaries) stop in the pelvis while the male gonads (testicles) continue their descent before birth to reach the scrotum through the inguinal canal. Even in the adult after the descent of the reproductive organ, these organs receive their nerve supply and blood supply from the Abdominal Aorta, which is in the area between the backbone (spinal column) and the ribs. Even the lymphatic drainage and the venous return goes to the same area.

HUMAN BEINGS CREATED FROM *NUTFAH* (Minute Quantity of Liquid)

The Glorious Qur'aan mentions no less than eleven times that the human being is created from *nutfa*h, which means a minute quantity of liquid or a trickle of liquid which remains after emptying a cup. This is mentioned in several verses of the Qur'aan including 22:5 and 23:13. [13]

Science has confirmed in recent times that only one out of an average of three million sperms is required for fertilising the ovum. This means that only a

[13] The same is also mentioned in the Qur'an in 16:4, 18:37, 35:11, 36:77, 40:67, 53:46, 75:37, 76:2 and 80:19.

1/three millionth part or 0.00003% of the quantity of sperms that are emitted is required for fertilisation.

HUMAN BEINGS CREATED FROM *SULALAH* (Quintessence of liquid)

"And made his progeny From a quintessence Of the nature of A fluid despised." [Al-Qur'aan 32:8]

The Arabic word *sulâlah* means quintessence or the best part of a whole. We have come to know now that only one single spermatozoon that penetrates the ovum is required for fertilization, out of the several millions produced by man. That one spermatozoon out of several millions, is referred to in the Qur'aan as *sulâla*h. *Sulâlah* also means gentle extraction from a fluid. The fluid refers to both male and female germinal fluids containing gametes. Both ovum and sperm are gently extracted from their environments in the process of fertilization.

MAN CREATED FROM *NUTFATUN AMSHAAJ*

(Mingled liquids)

Consider the following Qur'aanic verse: **"Verily We created Man from a drop Of mingled sperm."** [Al-Qur'aan 76:2]

The Arabic word *nutfatin amshaajin* means mingled liquids. According to some commentators of the Qur'aan, mingled liquids refers to the male or female agents or liquids. After mixture of male and female gamete, the zygote still remains *nutfa*h. Mingled liquids can also refer to spermatic fluid that is formed of various secretions that come from various glands.

Therefore *nutfatin amsa*j, i.e. a minute quantity of mingled fluids refers to the male and female gametes (germinal fluids or cells) and part of the surrounding fluids.

The Qur'aan and Modern Science: Compatible or Incompatible?

Distributed by AHYA Multi-Media http://www.ahya.org

SEX DETERMINATION

The sex of a fetus is determined by the nature of the sperm and not the ovum. The sex of the child, whether female or male, depends on whether the 23rd pair of chromosomes is XX or XY respectively. Primarily sex determination occurs at fertilization and depends upon the type of sex chromosome in the sperm that fertilizes an ovum. If it is an 'X' bearing sperm that fertilizes the ovum, the fetus is a female and if it is a 'Y' bearing sperm then the fetus is a male. **"That He did create In pairs – male and female, From a seed when lodged (In its place)."** [Al-Qur'aan 53:45-46]

The Arabic word *nutfah* means a minute quantity of liquid and *tumnâ* means ejaculated or planted. Therefore *nutfah* specifically refers to sperm because it is ejaculated. The Qur'aan says: **"Was he not a drop of sperm emitted (In lowly form)? "Then did he become A clinging clot; Then did (Allah) make And fashion (him) In due proportion. "And of him He made Two sexes, male And female."** [Al-Qur'aan 75:37-39]

Here again it is mentioned that a small quantity (drop) of sperm (indicated by the word *nutfatan min maniyyi*n) which comes from the man is responsible for the sex of the fetus.

Mothers-in-law in the Indian subcontinent, by and large prefer having male grandchildren and often blame their daughters-in-law if the child is not of the desired sex. If only they knew that the determining factor is the nature of the male sperm and not the female ovum! If they were to blame anybody, they should blame their sons and not their daughters-in-law since both the Qur'aan and Science hold that it is the male fluid that is responsible for the sex of the child!

FOETUS PROTECTED BY THREE VEILS OF DARKNESS

"He makes you, In the wombs of your mothers, In stages, one after another, In three veils of darkness." [Al-Qur'aan 39:6]

According to Prof. Keith Moore these three veils of darkness in the Qur'aan refer to:

(i) anterior abdominal wall of the mother
(ii) the uterine wall
(iii) the amnio-chorionic membrane.

EMBRYONIC STAGES

"Man We did create From a quintessence (of clay); Then We placed him

As (a drop of) sperm In a place of rest, firmly fixed; Then We made the sperm Into a clot of congealed blood; Then of that clot We made A (foetus) lump; then We Made out of that lump Bones and clothed the bones With flesh; then We developed Out of it another creature. So blessed be Allah, The Best to create!" [Al-Qur'aan 23:12-14]

In this verse Allah states that man is created from a small quantity of liquid which is placed in a place of rest, firmly fixed (well established or lodged) for which the Arabic word *qarârin makîn* is used.

The uterus is well protected from the posterior by the spinal column supported firmly by the back muscles. The embryo is further protected by the amniotic sac containing the amniotic fluid. Thus the foetus has a well protected dwelling place. This small quantity of fluid is made into *alaqa*h, meaning something which clings. It also means a leech-like substance. Both descriptions are scientifically acceptable as in the very early stages the foetus clings to the wall and also appears to resemble the leech in shape. It also behaves like a

leech (blood sucker) and acquires its blood supply from the mother through the placenta. The third meaning of the word *alaqah* is a blood clot. During

this *alaqah* stage, which spans the third and fourth week of pregnancy, the blood clots within closed vessels. Hence the embryo acquires the appearance of a blood clot in addition to acquiring the appearance of a leech. In 1677, Hamm and Leeuwenhoek were the first scientists to observe human sperm cells (spermatozoa) using a microscope. They thought that a sperm cell contained a miniature human being which grew in the uterus to form a newborn. This was known as the perforation theory. When scientists discovered that the ovum was bigger than the sperm, it was thought by De Graf and others that the foetus existed in a miniature form in the ovum. Later, in the 18th century Maupertuis propagated the theory of biparental inheritance. The *alaqah* is transformed into *mudghah* which means 'something that is chewed (having teeth marks)' and also something that is tacky and small which can be put in the mouth like gum. Both these explanations are scientifically correct. Prof. Keith Moore took a piece of plaster seal and made it into the size and shape of the early stage of foetus and chewed it between the teeth to make it into a 'Mudgha'. He compared this with the photographs of the early stage of foetus. The teeth marks resembled the 'somites' which is the early formation of the spinal column.

This *mudghah* is transformed into bones *(izâ*m). The bones are clothed with intact flesh or muscles *(lah*m). Then Allah makes it into another creature. Prof. Marshall Johnson is one of the leading scientists in US, and is the head of the Department of Anatomy and Director of the Daniel Institute at the Thomas Jefferson University in Philadelphia in US. He was asked to comment on the verses of the Qur'aan dealing with embryology. He said that the verses of the Qur'aan describing the embryological stages cannot be a coincidence. He said it was probable that Muhammad (pbuh) had a powerful microscope. On being reminded that the Qur'aan was revealed 1400 years ago, and microscopes were invented centuries after the time of Prophet

Muhammad (pbuh), Prof. Johnson laughed and admitted that the first microscope invented could not magnify more than 10 times and could not show a clear picture. Later he said: "I see nothing here in conflict with the concept that Divine intervention was involved when Muhammad (pbuh) recited the Qur'aan."

According to Dr. Keith Moore, the modern classification of embryonic development stages which is adopted throughout the world, is not easily comprehensible, since it identifies stages on a numerical basis i.e. stage I, stage II, etc. The divisions revealed in the Qur'aan are based on distinct and easily identifiable forms or shapes, which the embryo passes through. These are based on different phases of prenatal development and provide elegant scientific descriptions that are comprehensible and practical.

Similar embryological stages of human development have been described in the following verses: **"Was he not a drop Of sperm emitted (In lowly form)? Then did he become a clinging clot; Then did (Allah) make and fashion (him) In due proportion. And of him He made Two sexes, male and female."** [Al-Qur'aan 75:37-39]

"Him Who created thee, fashioned thee in due proportion, And gave thee a just bias; In whatever Form He wills, Does He put thee together." [Al-Qur'aan 82:7-8]

EMBRYO PARTLY FORMED AND PARTLY UNFORMED

At the *mugdhah* stage, if an incision is made in the embryo and the internal organ is dissected, it will be seen that most of them are formed while the others are not yet completely formed.

According to Prof. Johnson, if we describe the embryo as a complete creation, then we are only describing that part which is already created. If we describe it as an incomplete creation, then we are only describing that part which is not yet created. So, is it a complete creation or an incomplete creation? There is no better description of this stage of embryogenesis than the Qur'aanic description, "partly formed and partly unformed", as in the following verse:

"We created you Out of dust, then out of Sperm, then out of a leech-like Clot, then out of a morsel Of flesh, partly formed And partly unformed." [Al-Qur'aan 22:5]

Scientifically we know that at this early stage of development there are some cells which are differentiated and there are some cells that are undifferentiated – some organs are formed and yet others unformed.

SENSE OF HEARING AND SIGHT

The first sense to develop in a developing human embryo is hearing. The foetus can hear sounds after the 24th week. Subsequently, the sense of sight is developed and by the 28th week, the retina becomes sensitive to light. Consider the following Qur'aanic verses related to the development of the senses in the embryo: **"And He gave You (the faculties of) hearing and sight and feeling (And understanding)."** [Al-Qur'aan 32:9]

"Verily We created Man from a drop Of mingled sperm, In order to try him: So We gave him (the gifts), Of Hearing and Sight." [Al-Qur'aan

76:2]

"It is He Who has created For you (the faculties of) Hearing, sight, feeling And understanding: little thanks It is ye give!" [Al-Qur'aan 23:78]

In all these verses the sense of hearing is mentioned before that of sight. Thus the Qur'aanic description matches with the discoveries in modern embryology.

XII. GENERAL SCIENCE

FINGERPRINTS

"Does man think that We Cannot assemble his bones? Nay, We are able to put Together in perfect order The very tips of his fingers." [Al-Qur'aan 75:3-4]

Unbelievers argue regarding resurrection taking place after bones of dead people have disintegrated in the earth and how each individual would be identified on the Day of Judgement. Almighty Allah answers that He can not only assemble our bones but can also reconstruct perfectly our very fingertips.

Why does the Qur'aan, while speaking about determination of the identity of the individual, speak specifically about fingertips? In 1880, fingerprinting became the scientific method of identification, after research done by Sir Francis Golt. No two persons in the world can ever have exactly the same fingerprint pattern. That is the reason why police forces worldwide use fingerprints to identify the criminal. 1400 years ago, who could have known the uniqueness of each human's fingerprint? Surely it could have been none other than the Creator Himself!

PAIN RECEPTORS PRESENT IN THE SKIN

It was thought that the sense of feeling and pain was only dependent on the brain. Recent discoveries prove that there are pain receptors present in the skin without which a person would not be able to feel pain. When a doctor examines a patient suffering from burn injuries, he verifies the degree of burns by a pinprick. If the patient feels pain, the doctor is happy, because it indicates that the burns are superficial and the pain receptors are intact. On the other hand if the patient does not feel any pain, it indicates that it is a deep burn and the pain receptors have been destroyed. The Qur'aan gives an indication of the existence of pain receptors in the following verse: **"Those who reject Our signs, We shall soon Cast into the Fire; As often as their skins Are roasted through, We shall change them For fresh skins, That they may taste The Penalty: for Allah Is Exalted in Power, Wise."** [Al-Qur'aan 4:56]

Prof. Tagatat Tejasen, Chairman of the Department of Anatomy at Chiang Mai University in Thailand, has spent a great amount of time on research of pain receptors. Initially he could not believe that the Qur'aan mentioned this scientific fact 1,400 years ago. He later verified the translation of this particular Qur'aanic verse. Prof. Tejasen was so impressed by the scientific accuracy of the Qur'aanic verse, that at the 8th Saudi Medical Conference held in Riyadh on the Scientific Signs of Qur'aan and Sunnah he proclaimed in public: "There is no God but Allah and Muhammad (pbuh) is His Messenger."

The Qur'aan and Modern Science: Compatible or Incompatible?

Distributed by AHYA Multi-Media http://www.ahya.org

CONCLUSION

To attribute the presence of scientific facts in the Qur'aan to coincidence would be against common sense and a true scientific approach. The Qur'aan invites all humans to reflect on the Creation of this universe in the verse: **"Behold! In the creation Of the heavens and the earth, And the alternation Of Night and Day – There are indeed Signs For men of understanding."** [Al-Qur'aan 3:190]

The scientific evidences of the Qur'aan clearly prove its Divine Origin. No human could have produced a book, fourteen hundred years ago, that would contain profound scientific facts, to be discovered by humankind centuries later. The Qur'aan, however, is not a book of Science but a book of 'Signs'. These signs invite Man to realize the purpose of his existence on earth, and to live in harmony with Nature. The Qur'aan is truly a message from Allah, the Creator and Sustainer of the universe. It contains the same message of the Oneness of God, that was preached by all prophets, right from Adam, Moses, Jesus to Muhammad (peace be upon them).

Several detailed tomes have been written on the subject of Qur'aan and modern science and further research in this field is on. Inshallah, this research will help mankind to come closer to the Word of the Almighty. This booklet contains only a few of the scientific facts present in the Qur'aan. I cannot claim to have done full justice to the subject. Prof. Tejasen accepted Islam on the strength of just one scientific 'sign' mentioned in the Qu'ran. Some people may require ten signs while some may require hundred signs to be convinced about the Divine Origin of the Qur'aan. Some would be unwilling to accept the Truth even after being shown a thousand signs. The Qur'aan condemns such a closed mentality in the verse: **"Deaf, dumb and blind, They will not return (To the path)."** [Al-Qur'aan 2:18]

The Qur'aan contains a complete code of life for the individual and society. Alhamdulillah (Praise be to Allah), the Qur'aanic way of life is far superior to the 'isms' that modern man has invented out of sheer ignorance. Who can give better guidance than the Creator Himself?

I pray that this humble effort is accepted by Allah, to whom I pray for mercy and guidance (Aameen).

God forbids you not, with regards to those who fight you not for (your) faith nor drive you out of your homes, from dealing kindly and justly with them; for God loveth those who are just (Qur'an, 60:8)

Additional information on science & hadiths: hadiths are some teachings of prophet Muhammad (pbuh)

Muhammad & science: "If you hear of an outbreak of plague in a land, do not enter it; but if the plague breaks out in a place while you are in it, do not leave that

place." The Prophet (peace be upon him) said: "If you hear of an outbreak of plague in a land, do not enter it; but if the plague breaks out in a place while you are in it, do not leave that place."

(Reported by al-Bukhari and Muslim.)

Also, he (peace be upon him) said: "He who runs away from the place of plague is like the one running away from fighting in the cause of Allah; and he who is patient and stays where he is, he will be rewarded with the reward of a martyr." (Reported by Ahmad.)

The Scientific Fact:

Modern science now understands the ways in which microorganisms multiply and the diseases they cause. Scientists affirm that healthy people who have no symptoms in the place of plague are already carrying the microbe and so they represent a real threat because they may transfer the plague to another place if they move to it.

Thus, this system of quarantine, in which all the people of the city that suffers from plague are prevented from leaving, and visitors are also prevented from entering, has now been established worldwide. In the 15th century, plague hit Europe causing the death of a quarter of its citizens. At that time, plagues and contagious diseases were much less in the Muslim world.

Facets of Scientific Inimitability:

At the time of the Prophet (peace be upon him) as well as before and after his time until Pasteur managed to discover the existence of microbes, people used to think that diseases were caused by devils, demons, and stars. That is they were not related to cleanliness or certain behaviors; thus, they resorted to sorcery and magic as a remedy.

In such an environment, the Prophet (peace be upon him) established the system of quarantine which is considered the basis of modern preventative medicine after the discovery of the microbes that cause diseases and plagues. The Prophet (peace be upon him) ordered his Companions: "If you hear of an outbreak of plague in a land, do not enter it; but if the plague breaks out in a place while you are in it, do not leave that place." In order to make sure that his order would be carried out properly, he (peace be upon him) established a wall around the area of the plague and promised those who are patient and stay in the area of the plague with the reward of the martyrs, and those who run away from it were promised doom and perdition. Thus, he (peace be upon him) said: "He who runs away from the place of the plague is like the one running away from fighting in the cause of Allah and he who forbears it and stays where he is, he will be rewarded with the reward of a martyr."

If a healthy person was asked two hundred years ago to stay with the sick people in a plague area, he would have considered this some kind of nonsense and in response to his desire to live he would have run away to another place. Only Muslims did not run away and leave at the time of plague in compliance with the order of the Prophet (peace be upon him). Non-Muslims mocked them for this act until it was later discovered that those who appear to be healthy with no symptoms, are the germ carriers who might transfer the plague to another place if they moved to it. They would move freely and mingle with healthy people, so they might cause them to catch the disease.

Who told the Prophet (peace be upon him) this fact? Could a human being know something like this fourteen centuries ago, or is it revelation from the All-Knowing, the Almighty Allah. Allah, the Almighty, says:

[And say, O Muhammad, to these polytheists and pagans, 'All the praises and thanks be to Allah. He will show you His signs and you shall recognize them. And your Lord is not unaware of what you do.'] (An-Naml: 93)

Sunnah & Science

By: admin

Abu Mas'ud (A.S.) narrated that Allah's Messenger said:

"The sun and the moon do not eclipse because of someone's death but they are two signs amongst the signs of Allah. Whenever you see these eclipses invoke Allah, pray, exclaim, (Allah is Most Great) and give charity."

'A'ishah (A.S.) narrated that, "There was a solar eclipse during the life-time of Allah's Messenger (PBUH). The Prophet (PBUH) led the people in prayer, and stood up and performed a lengthy recital during the prayer. Then bowed for a long while (made a long *Ruku*). He stood up again and performed another long recital of the Qur'an, but this time the period of standing (*Qiyam*) was shorter than the first one. He bowed again for a long time but shorter than the first one (*Ruku*), then he prostrated and prolonged the prostration. He did the same in the second *Rak'ah* as he did in the first and then finished the prayer. By then the sun (eclipse) had cleared. He delivered the *Khutbah* (sermon) and after praising and glorifying Allah, he said:

"The sun and the moon are two signs from amongst Allah's signs and they do not eclipse because of the death or life of anyone. Therefore, whenever you see an eclipse, remember Allah and say Takbir (exclaim, Allah is Most Great), pray and give Sadaqah (charity)."

Explanation of the Hadith

A solar eclipse occurs when the moon passes between the sun and the earth, which causes a total or partial solar eclipse. A total eclipse takes place in a limited zone on that part of the earth directly facing the sun, at which the sunlight dims to resemble bright moonlight within a few minutes. To the north and south of this band or zone, a partial eclipse takes place. The part of the sun, which eclipses keep getting smaller as we get away from the total eclipse band towards the direction of the two poles.

The Prophet (PBUH) says in this Hadith:

"The sun and the moon do not eclipse because of the death or life (i.e. the birth) of someone but they are two signs amongst the signs of Allah."

This means that they are two cosmic phenomena, which frequently occur, regardless of the death or life (i.e. birth) of anyone, contrary to what some people used to claim in the Arab

Peninsula and other parts of the world. They used to relate the occurrence of these cosmic phenomena to the birth or death of a great person. The Prophet (PBUH) in this Hadith totally denies all of these superstitions, and assures that they are cosmic phenomena, which recur frequently.

Islam deals with ECLIPSE as cosmic phenomena

Science has proven that the moon is followed by a conical shadow, called the umbra, as it blocks the sunrays. In its movement around the earth, the moon's conical shadow passes along with it. At the time of conjunction, which occurs once every lunar month, the moon falls exactly in the middle between the sun and the earth, thus blocking its light totally or partially. Nevertheless, in most of the lunar months, the moon's shadow does not reach the earth, while passing between it and the sun and in such case the sunlight is not blocked. Hence, no eclipse takes place. That is why total solar eclipses are very rare. Sometimes during a solar eclipse the moon falls in the middle between the earth and the sun, and the visible sun narrows to a thin crescent, and the corona appears. At the moment before totality, brilliant points of light, called Baily's beads, flash out.

When the total eclipse takes place, the sky becomes completely dark and the stars become visible in the middle of the day. So in a few minutes, broad daylight turns into what looks like the night, which causes a feeling of panic and depression, not only for human beings, but for all creatures. Birds shelter in their nests, and animals hide in their dens, or get into a state of cautious stillness.

As for the lunar eclipse, it takes place when the earth, being between the sun and the moon, casts a long, conical shadow, called the umbra, with an area of partial shadow called the penumbra around it. This is a phenomenon, which can be observed from all parts of the earth. In most months, the moon passes above or under the umbra, the conical shadow of the earth, and does not enter it. Thus, the lunar eclipse does not take place. During the solar eclipse, the solar energy that reaches the earth decreases and hence the temperature of the earth drops. However, during the lunar eclipse, the solar energy, which reaches the earth increases, causing the temperature of the earth to relatively increase for a few minutes. Since these phenomena are very accurately calculated, the earth is exposed to extreme dangers that only Allah knows how grave they are. That is why the Prophet (PBUH) asked Muslims to invoke Allah, the Almighty, praise Him, exclaim, "Allah is Most Great", and glorify Him. Moreover, the Prophet asked Muslims to pray and pay charity, praying that Allah will protect the earth and its inhabitants from these dangers.

This is the reason why the Prophet (PBUH) said in other narrations of the same Hadith: *"Rush to prayer"* and in another narration he said:

"These signs sent by Allah do not occur because of the life or death of somebody, but Allah frightens His worshippers with them. So when you see anything thereof, rush to invoke Allah, pray to Him and ask for His forgiveness."

One cannot help wondering how the Prophet (PBUH) could attain such accurate scientific facts, more than fourteen hundred years ago, at a time when people were up to their ears in superstitions and myths. It really is an explicit proof of the Prophet's Divine Message.

Sunnah & Science

By: Dr. Zaghloul El-Naggar

THE SUN: NEVER CEASE NOR DISAPPEAR

Ibn 'Abbas (R.A.) narrated that the Prophet (PBUH) was asked: "Where does the sun set, and where does it rise from? The Messenger of Allah (PBUH) answered, "It is going in a (nonstop) regular motion; it does not cease or disappear. It sets in one place and rises in another, and sets in another place and rises elsewhere and so on. So, some people would say the sun has set and others would say it has just risen (at the same moment)."

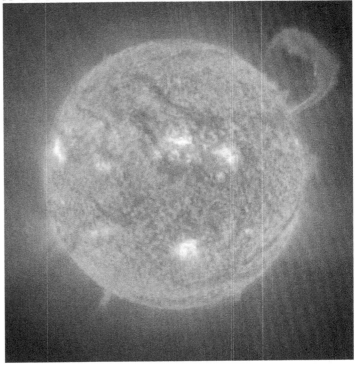

Explanation of the Hadith

This hadith refers to the fact that there is a continuous alternate sunrise and sunset on earth. This could only take place if the earth is spherical or spheroid, and is, at the same time, continuously rotating round its axis facing the sun. This motion pattern leads to the continuous alternation of day and night on its surface, until life on earth comes to an end, i.e. until the Day of Resurrection.

One of the most prominent phenomena linked to this spherical shape of the earth, is that there are different places of sunrise and sunset for different zones of the globe. Each of the sun, the moon and other celestial bodies, sets somewhere in the globe and rises in another. They are all rotating, regularly, in fixed orbits, which they never leave or depart from. Truly, Allah says:

(...They all float, each in an orbit.) (Surat Ya-Sin: 40).

The Messenger of Allah (PBUH) talked about all these cosmic facts in such accurate scientific style at a period of time when people thought that the earth was flat and stationary. This is definitely one of the signs, which testifies to the truthfulness of the message of Muhammad (PBUH). For sure, no one in the Arabian Peninsula at the time of revelation, and for centuries to follow realized the fact that the earth is spherical and that it rotates around its axis facing the sun. Needless to say that at that time, no one was able to perceive the real or the apparent motion of the moon, the sun and other celestial bodies, as Arabia was but a simple and primitive environment.

The Glorious Qur'an refers to the spherical shape of the earth and its axial rotating, and to its revolving in its orbit around the sun. The Qur'an refers to these issues in many verses but in a subtle implicit way which may not astound the Bedouins in the desert of the Arabian Peninsula at the time of revelation, but still keeps the scientific fact in context.

Sun does not cease or disappear

Among these verses are the following:

Allah the Almighty says:

(He has created the heavens and the earth with truth. He makes the night to go in the day and makes the day to go in the night. And He has subjected the sun and the moon. Each running (on a fixed course) for an appointed term. Verily, He is the All-Mighty, the oft-Forgiving.) (Surat Az-Zumar (The Groups):5)

1. The Glorious Qur'an also confirms in more than one verse that the earth is "spread out" without ending at an edge. This could only be possible if the earth is spherical or spheroid, as the spherical shape is the only shape, which could endlessly be spread out or extended. For example, Allah the Almighty says:

(And it is He Who spread out the earth, and placed therein firm mountains and rivers...) (Surat Ar-Ra'd (The Thunder): 3)

2. The same fact is also assured when the Qur'an refers to the East and the West in different forms. First in the singular, then in the dual form by indicating that there are "Two Easts and Two Wests", and in the plural form by referring to "Easts and Wests". This also emphasizes the fact that the earth is spherical and that it rotates round its axis while facing the sun. These verses also emphasize the fact that the Earth is tilted on its axis and that it does not orbit the sun in a perfect circle.

3. The fact that the earth is spherical in shape is also emphasized by the verses referring to the alternation of night and day. The Glorious Qur'an indicates how Allah makes the 'Night overlap (Kawwar) the Day and the Day overlap the Night' (Surat Az-Zumar: 5). Among the verses that indicate the spherical shape of the earth is the one referring to the passing away of the mountains in the same way the clouds do:

(And you will see the mountains and think them solid, but they shall pass away as the passing away of the clouds...) (Surat An-Naml (The Ants):88)

All of the above facts mentioned in the Qur'an have urged Muslims, at the time of the Abbasid Caliph al-Ma'mun, to measure the circumference of the earth very accurately. Their motive was the firm belief that the earth is spherical and that it rotates around its axis facing the sun. Moreover, the Muslim scholar and scientist "al-Bayyruni" divided the earth into lines of longitude and latitude, in his book:" Tahdid Nihayat al-Amakin li Tas-hih Masafat al-Masakin," which he wrote in 416 A.H (about 1040 A.C.).

The source of all this knowledge is the illuminating signs that are mentioned in the Qur'an and Sunnah of the Prophet (PBUH), and each of them testifies to the truthfulness and the Divine nature of the Message of the last of the Prophets and Messengers. This accurate scientific knowledge could not be obtained except for a Divine Revelation.

Sunnah & Science

By: Dr. Zaghloul El-Naggar

THE MOON CLEFT ASUNDER

Anas ibn Malik (A.S.) narrated that the people of Makkah asked the Prophet (PBUH) to show them a miracle, so he showed them the splitting of the moon, into two distinct parts, that they even saw the mountain of Hira' between them.

Explanation of the Hadith

This incident was narrated by a number of the companions of the Prophet (PBUH), among them were: 'Abdullah ibn 'Umar, 'Abdullah ibn Abbas and others. The Indian and Chinese calendars have recorded the incident of the splitting of the moon.

Artistic impression of moon splitting by Prophet Muhammad (SAAS)

A few years ago while I was giving a lecture at the Faculty of Medicine at Cardiff University, in Wales, a Muslim asked me a question about the verses at the beginning of Surat al-Qamar (the moon), about the splitting of the moon, and whether it is considered as one of the scientific signs which are mentioned in the Qur'an and whether there is any scientific evidence discovered to explain this incident.

My answer was that this incident is considered one of the most tangible miracles, which took place to support the Prophet (PBUH) when he was challenged by the polytheists and disbelievers of Quraish, showing them this miracle to prove that he is a Messenger of Allah. Anyway, miracles take place as unusual incidents that break all regular laws of nature. Therefore, conventional science is unable to explain how miracles take place, and if they were not mentioned in the Qur'an and in the Sunnah of the Prophet (PBUH), we would not have been obliged to believe in them. Therefore, we believe that the incident of the splitting of the moon took place exactly as the words of Allah Glorified be Who says:

(The Hour has drawn near , and the moon has been cleft asunder . And if they see a sign, they turn away, and say: (This is continuous magic). They belied (this Qur'an), and followed their own lusts. And every matter will be settled [according to the kind of deeds (for the doer of good deeds, his deeds will take him to Paradise, and similarly evil deeds will take their doers to Hell)]. And indeed there has come to them news (in this Qur'an) wherein there is (enough warning) to check (them from evil), Perfect wisdom (this Qur'an), but (the preaching of) warners benefit them not.) (Surat Al-Qamar (The Moon): 1-5)

When I finished my speech, a British man from the audience named Dawud Musa Pidcock, leader of the British Muslim Party, asked to add something to my answer. He said: "It is these verses, at the beginning of surat al-Qamar that made me embrace Islam in the late seventies." This occurred while he was doing extensive research in comparative religion, and one of the Muslims gave him a copy of translation of the meanings of the Qur'an. When he opened this copy for the first time, he came across Surat al-Qamar, and he read the verses at the beginning of the surah, and could not believe that the moon had split into two distinct parts and they were rejoined, so he closed the copy of the translation and kept it aside.

In 1978 Mr. Pidcock was destined by Allah's Will to watch a program about space journeys, in which the well-known British announcer Jamed Burke, received three of the American space scientists. During the debate, the announcer kept criticizing the immoderate spending by NASA (millions of Dollars) on space projects, while there are millions of people on earth suffering from starvation, diseases and ignorance. The answer of the space experts came to assert that it was these journeys that made it feasible to develop important technology applied in medical diagnosis and treatment, industry, agriculture, and many other fields. During this debate, they referred to the first time that a human being landed on the surface of the moon, and how this trip cost more than $100 million dollars. The scientists went on to say that this journey proved a scientific fact, that if they had spent several times as much as they did to convince people with it, no body would have believed them. This fact was that the moon had been split a long time ago and rejoined, and there is a lot of concrete evidence on the surface of the moon to prove this.

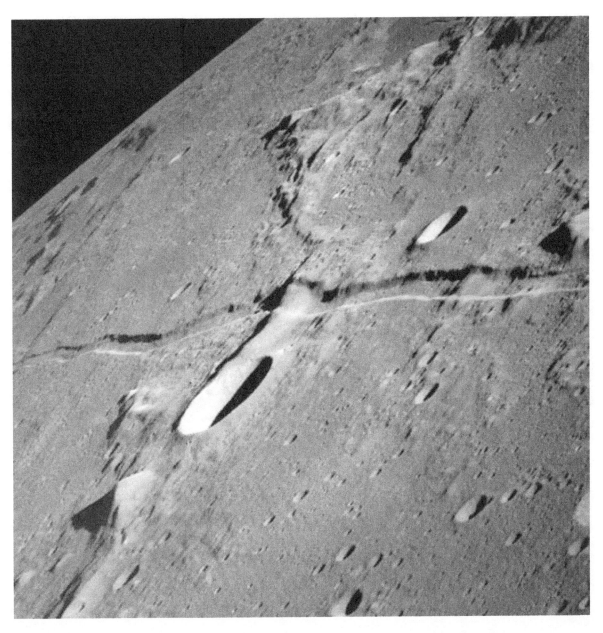

This oblique view of the Moon's surface was photographed by the Apollo 10 astronauts in May

1969. Center point coordinates are located at 13 degrees, 3 minutes east longitude and 7 degrees, minute north latitude. One of the Apollo 10 astronauts attached a 250mm lens and aimed a handhel 70mm camera at the surface from lunar orbit for a series of pictures in this area.

Mr. Pidcock went on to say : " When I heard this , I jumped off my chair , and said this is a miracle which took place fourteen hundred years ago to support

Muhammad , and the Qur'an narrates it in such a detailed way . After this long period and during the age of science and technology, Allah employs people (non-Muslims) who spent all this money for nothing but to prove that this miracle had actually happened. Then, I said to myself, this must be the true religion, and I went back to the translation of the meanings of the Qur'an, reading it eagerly. It was these verses at the opening of surat al-Qamar that lie behind my reversion to Islam."

The Hour has drawn near , and the moon has been cleft asunder)

(surat Al-Qamar (The Moon): 1-2)

This happens at a time when some Muslims claim that the splitting of the moon has not yet taken place, and that it is one of the signs of the Hereafter as the opening of the surah says: (The Hour has drawn near.) They are oblivious to the fact that the Prophet (PBUH) said in a hadith narrated by Imam Muslim , on the authority of Sahl ibn Sa'd that Sahl said : "I heard the Messenger of Allah (PBUH) say :

"I and the Last Hour are (close to each other) like this (and he pointed by joining his forefinger, (one) next to the thumb and the middle finger (together)."

Those who deny the incident of the splitting of the moon, use incorrect evidence to support their opinion as they use the verse in surat al-Isra:

(And nothing stops Us from sending the evidences (proofs , signs) but that the people of old denied them.)

(Surat Al-Isrâ' (The Journey by Night): 59)

This verse is not used in the right context since many perceptible signs and miracles took place during the noble life of the Prophet (PBUH).

Peace and blessings of Allah be upon the seal of Prophets (PBUH) , for whom Allah made the moon split into two parts , twice , as an honor for him and to raise his rank and support his message (among his people) , and left for us a concrete evidence to prove that this splitting did actually take place .

Sunnah & Science

By: Dr. Zaghloul El-Naggar

Unleashing the Treasures of Islam

(Please review these questions, it might sound offensive but it's a way to reveal the truth if you really believe in God read the Quran and bible and ask these questions to the church, priests & your self so you can find out what is truth about God & what are against the truth from God.Dont get emotional or angry but think with cool brain what is really real & the only truth of God. Dare to explore, dare to ask & dare to know. God is truth & truth is above all.Faisal)

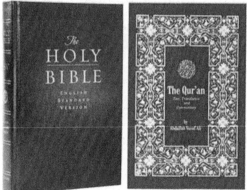

By Abdalla S. Alothman

101 Proofs that the Quran is Not Copied from the Bible

In the Name of Allah,
the Most Compassionate,
the Ever Merciful

{Do they not then think deeply in the Qur'ân, or are their hearts locked up (from understanding it)?} **[Quran 47:24]**

{Nay, We fling (send down) the truth (this Qur'ân) against the falsehood (disbelief), so it destroys it, and behold, it (falsehood) is vanished. And woe to you for that (lie) which you ascribe (to Us)}. [**Quran 21:18**]

Time and time again, we Muslims have to endure accusations that our Qur'an is copied from the Bible. Below are 101 proofs that makes it impossible for the Qur'an to be copied from the Bible.

1 - Who was created first, Adam or Satan? The Quran says Satan, the Bible doesn't say anything.

2 - Who was created first, Adam or the Angles? The Quran says the Angels, the Bible doesn't say anything.

3 - Why doesn't the Bible mention that Noah had two wives, one was disobedient, and she died. And another which was saved.

4 - Why does the Bible say that Noah's ark is in Ararat but it was discovered in Al-Judyy, as the Quran says so?

5 - Why does the Bible say that God afflicted women for Eve's sin, and the Quran doesn't tell us such thing.

6 - Where does the Bible tell us about the story of Aad and Thamood ? The town of Thamoud has been discovered in Saudi Arabia–it's located in a place called Mada-in Saleh. And recently, the town of Aad has been discovered with the help of NASA's satellites. Check the link : http://www.pbs.org/wgbh/nova/ubar/

7 - Where does the Bible mention Prophet Saleh ?

8 - Where does the Bible mention Prophet Huud ?

9 - Where does the Bible mention Prophet Shu'ayb ?

10 - Where does the Bible refer to Al-Khidr ?

11 - Where does the Bible mention Luqmaan ?

12 - Why doesn't the Bible mention the story of the Cow that happened between Moses and the Jews.

13 - Where do you find in the Quran any reference to Hosea, Malachi, Micha, Jude, Nahum, Nehemiah, Obadaiah, Esther, Joel, Ruth, etc ?

14 - Why doesn't the Bible mention the story of Thul-Qarnayn.

15 - Why doesn't the Bible mention the story of the People of the Cave?.

16 - Why doesn't the Bible mention the story of Antioch in Surat Yasin?.

17 - Why does the Bible say that Jesus was crucified, and the Quran says that he was saved?

18 - Why does the Bible say that Abraham sacrificed his only begotten son, Isaac, and forgets that he had another son called Ishamael, who is older than Isaac?.

19 - Regarding the dream Joseph had in Genesis 37, why is it fulfilled in the Quran and not fulfilled in the Bible? Could it be because that Joseph's mother died before Joseph had his dream? Bad prophecy.

20 - Why is it that the Bible tells us that the Holy Spirit had sex with Mary, and the Quran tells us that the Angel who visited Mary told her that she will bear a son, and he is ONLY informing her of what God has decreed?

21 - Why is it that the Bible tells us that Moses was adopted by Pharaoh's daughter, and the Quran tells us it was Pharaoh's wife?.

22 – Why is it that the Quran tells us that Lut was a pious prophet, and the Bible tells us that he had sex with his daughters?

23 - Why is it that the Quran tells us in Sura 19 and 20 that Moses was a special chosen prophet who was raised under God's supervision, and the Bible tells us that he died because he didn't disobeyed God?

24 - Why is it that the Bible says that it is written with the false pen of the scribe in Jeremiah 8:8, and the Quran tells us that it has no discrepancies?

55   **25 -** Why is it that the Bible tells us that Pharaoh did not drown, and the Quran tells us that he drowned, but Allah left his body as a sign to mankind. When they dissected Pharaoh's body, they found out that his body had too much salt inside it. You say the Quran is copied from the Bible? I say you are ignorant! Read the Quran 10:92.

26 – Why does the Bible tells us in Genesis that God had to take a walk to find Adam, and the Quran tells us that God's knowledge doesn't require that He walks?

27 - Why is it that the Quran tells us that Jesus spoke in the cradle, but the Bible knows nothing about the childhood of Jesus?

28 - Why is it that the Quran tells us that Jesus made miracles by giving life to statues made from clay?

29 - The Quran tells us that Aaron is innocent; he did not make the golden calf, but a man called Al-Samirri (A person who organizes songs and joy) made it, while the Bible tells us that Aaron made the Golden calf.

30 - why is it that the Quranic Laws state that the thief's hands should be chopped, and the laws of Moses say something else?

31 – Why does the Quran say lash the fornicators 100 times, and the Bible says stone them.

32 - Why does the Quran orders us to fast in Ramadhan and the Bible doesn't.

33 - Why does the Quran tells us that the inheritance share of the man is as twice as much as the woman, and the Bible has no such law?

34 - Why does the Quran tells us not to transgress in wars, and the Bible teaches us to kill every living thing including plants (Joshua 6).

35 - The Bible teaches us to kill unbelievers, and leave to ourselves YOUNG virgins who never knew a man (Numbers 31). Why isn't such thing present in the Quran?

36 - The Quran tells us to free slaves to enter heaven in Surat Al-Balad. Why doesn't the Bible say such thing?

37 - Why is Satan called a FALLEN ANGEL in the Bible, and not in the Quran?

38 – Why does the Quran tells us there are Jinn (Some are good and others are bad), but the Bible doesn't mention Jinn?

39 – Why is it that the Quran tells us to perform Hajj to Makkah, and the Bible doesn't tell us such thing?

40 – Why does the Quran tells us that Abraham and Ishmael built the Kaaba, while the Bible says no such thing?

41 - Why is it that the Bible condemns David as a murderer, and the Quran tells us that he was a pious sinless prophet?

42 - Why doesn't the Bible tell us the story of Solomon and Balqees?

43 - Why doesn't the Bible tell us that Solomon had Jinns who worked for him, and the Quran says so?

44 - Why is it that the Quran tells us that Solomon had soldiers from the Jinn and the Bible doesn't say so?

45 - Why is it that the Quran tells us that Solomon understood the speech of the birds and the Bible doesn't say so?

46 – Why is it that the Quran tells us that Solomon understood the speech of the ants and the Bible doesn't say so?

47 - Why is it that the Quran tells us that ONLY female bees get the honey, and the Bible doesn't say so?

48 – Why is it that the Quran tells us that the Quran mentions different levels in Paradise, and the Bible doesn't say so?

49 - Why is it that the Quran tells us that there is a tree in hell called Zaqquum, and the Bible doesn't say so?

50 - The Quran mentions Thal-Kifl as one of the prophets. Can you find his name in the Bible?

51 - Why is it that the Quran was finalized and approved by Prophet Mohammad (s), and the Bible was never approved by any prophet?

52 – Why didn't Mohammad make the Quran in chronological order just like the Bible? Why doesn't the Quran include the boring genealogies that are all over the Bible?

53 - Why is it that the Quran mentions Ishmael as an honorable prophet, and the Bible refers to him as the son of the slave woman (Galatians 4)?

54 - Why doesn't the Quran mention the story of the people of Tyre, while the Bible does?

55 - Why doesn't the Quran mentions the story of David and how he killed one of his enemies to marry his wife as the Bible did in I Samuel 25?

56 - Why is it that the Bible does not mention the story of David and Solomon with the sheep, and the Quran does?

57 - Why does the Bible mention Abraham's father by name, and the Quran mentions him by his nick?

58 - Why doesn't the Bible mention the story when Abraham was put into a fire by his people and the Quran does?

59 - Why doesn't the Quran mention the interesting events that happened to Abraham in Egypt? (See BONUS #15 for one amazing example.)

60 - Why is it that the Bible tells us that John's mother was the daughter of Aaron, and the Quran doesn't say so?

61 - Why doesn't the Bible mention the story of how Mary was raised, and the Quran does?

62 - Why doesn't the Quran and the Bible have the same story about the birth of Jesus? The Quran says that he was born under the remnants of a palm tree, but the Bible says he was born in a stable.

63 - According to the Bible, who are the Sabians?

64 – Where does the Bible mention the Magians?

65 - In Genesis, the Bible tells us that Jacob had a fight with God, and the Quran tells us in Surat Al-Baqara that whoever takes the Angels as enemies, he becomes an enemy of God. Why do we see this contradiction? Moreover, why didn't Mohammad (s) tell us that Jacob wrestled with God?

66 - Why is it that the Quran tells us in Surat Taaha that the staff of Moses became a REAL snake, and the Bible tells us that it only appeared to be a snake?

67 - Why is it that Moses was the one who threw his staff during the contest with the magicians, and the Bible tells us that Aaron is the one who threw it?

68 - The story of Moses and the bronze snake in Numbers 21 is pretty interesting. Why is it mentioned in the Bible and not in the Quran?

69 - The Quran tells us to follow a certain procedure to cleanse ourselves before prayers in 4:43. Why doesn't the Bible give us the same instructions?

70 - The Quran tells us that Earth is round, but the Bible tells us that the Earth is flat. Why?

71 – The Quran tells us about Haroot and Maroot in Surat Al-Baqara. Who are those characters according to the Bible?

72 – Why is the story of Gog and Magog different in the Quran and the Bible?

73 - The Bible tells us that Prophet Elijah was raised to God. Why doesn't the Quran say the same thing?

74 - The Bible tells us that Solomon had many wives. Why doesn't the Quran say the same thing?

75 – The Bible tells us that God RESTED after he created the world. The Quran says that nothing makes God tired. Why?

76 - The Quran details embryology, why doesn't the Bible?

77 - The Quran mentions the names of the Gods during Noah's time in Surat Nuuh, why aren't those names present in the Bible?

78 - The Bible tells us that the whole Earth was flooded, why doesn't the Quran say the same thing?

79 – The Quran tells us that hell has 7 doors in Surat Al-Hijr (Ch. 15), why doesn't the Bible mention such thing?

80 - Why does the Quran say that Lot's wife was a bad woman, but God punishes Lot's wife in the Bible just for accidentally turning back to see what was happening in Sodom?

81 - Why does the Bible accuse Noah for getting drunk in Genesis 9, and the Quran frees him from such accusation?

82 - Anyone who curses his mother shall be put to death, according to Leviticus 20, why don't we find such a law in the Quran?

83 - Why is it that apostates are killed according to the Bible, and not killed according to the Quran? See http://www.systemoflife.com/answering-islamophobes/abul-kasem/235-refuting-muhammad-said-death-converting-to-other-religion

84 – Why is it that tattoos are forbidden in the Bible (Leviticus 19), and no tattoos are mentioned in the Quran?

85 – The Quran instructs us to treat those who are born from an illegal sexual intercourse as Brothers. But the Bible tells us in Leviticus 23 that they should NOT even enter the assembly of the Lord. Why didn't Mohammad (s) copy this beautiful law?

86 – The Bible tells us in Deuteronomy 25, that if two men were beating up each other, and the wife of one of them interfered, she should have her hand chopped off. Why didn't Mohammad (s) copy this beautiful law?

87 - Why does the Bible encourage Bribery in Proverbs 17, and the Quran never encourages such thing?

88 – Why does the Bible say that wisdom is a source of sorrow in Ecclesiastes 1:18, and the Quran calls wisdom a gift in 2:269?

89 - Why does God in the Quran tells us to avoid bloodshed, and the Bible God curses the sword which doesn't do bloodshed (Jeremiah 48)?

90 - When God told Zachariah that he will have a son, Zachariah asked for a sign, and God gave him a sign in Sura 19. Does the Bible mention that sign? The Bible says that he could not speak, but it's detailed to us in the Sunnah that he was able to speak when he was praying. But, when it came to communicating with others, he did so by signs. Further more, the Bible says that Zakariyya was not able to speak because he was punished by Gabriel because he did not believe the angel, while the Quran tells us that it was a sign given to him–he asked God for a sign, and God gave him a sign, not a punishment.

91 - The Bible God in Leviticus 21 tells us that hunchbacks, dwarfs, cripples, blind people, people who are deformed or disfigured, or have damaged testicles–all those people cannot become priests. The Quran tells us that there is no difference between a man and another except in piety. Why didn't Mohammad (s) copy this BEAUTIFUL law from the Bible?

92 - Why does the Bible God in Leviticus 21 forbid priests from marrying divorced women, and the Quran doesn't say such thing?

93 - Why is it that the Bible tells the people to call a person who doesn't listen to his father or mother "stubborn and a drunkard"? The Quran does not tell us that we should call a person who is disobedient to his parents as a drunkard. Furthermore, the Biblical law is that this person should be stoned to death, but the Quran approves no such thing. Why?

94 - The Quran tells us that we are not above the Law. We must adhere to the Laws of God. But the Bible God tells the Christians in Galatians 2 that they are under no LAW!! In other words, God made all these laws, so that Christians can see them and smile. Why didn't Mohammad tell his people that the Quranic laws are only for non-Muslims?

95 - The Bible God tells us that He will let us see the sex organs of the Jews, but the Quran mentions no such thing. Mohammad (s) had serious problems with the Jews, so why didn't he make fun of them with something similar with what we read in Nahum 3?

96 - In Romans 6, the Bible tells us that Jesus will never die again. But The Quran tells us that he will die and he will be raised at Judgment day. Why didn't Mohammad copy from Romans 6?

97 - The Bible teaches Christians to drink wine, the Quran forbids Muslims drinking. Why?

98 - 1 Corinthians 6 tells us that our bodies are members of Christ. The Quran tells us that our bodies belong to Allah, Christ has nothing to do with our bodies. Why didn't Mohammad (s) copy that from the Bible?

99 - In Ezekiel 20, the Bible God tells us that he wanted to decimate all the Israelites, but He didn't do so because it would hurt his reputation. In the Quran God tells us that He does indeed take away all the people if they were wrongful (Like the people of Noah, Sodom, Aad, and Thamood) if He wills.

100 - The Bible God has a beautiful punishment in Malachi 2. He threatens an Israelite that He would fill his face with feces!! In the Quran, God never says such things.

101 - The Bible says that the Original Sin was committed by Adam and Eve when they ate from the forbidden tree. The Quran tells us that the Original Sin was Satan's arrogance when he didn't obey God, when God ordered him to do So.

BONUS:

1 - The Quran tells us about an argument in 2:258 about Abraham and the King. Does the Bible have this story?

2 – The Quran handles divorce with care. A divorced woman stays in her house; a man should provide for her; a man should not return his wife to give her a hard time, etc. Does the Bible have the same laws regarding divorce as the Quran?

3 - The Quran tells us that Sins are not inherited. But, the Bible tells us that sins are inherited.

4 – The Quran tells us that God forgave Adam's sin after he ate from the forbidden tree. Does the Bible say that?

5 - The Quran tells us in Sura 36, that the sun and the moon are independent from one another. Does the Bible say such thing?

6 - In 25:53 and 55:19-20 the Quran tells us about how salty and pure water bodies mix. Does the Bible say such thing?

7 - In Islam we believe that there are signs to Judgment Day. Most of these signs are mentioned in the Sunnah, however, one interesting sign is a Beast/animal that would appear to the people and inform them of their status. We find this beast mentioned in the Quran in 27:82. Does the Bible say such thing?

8 - The Quran tells us that man and women are created from ONE SOUL. Does the Bible say that man and women are created from one soul? No, the Bible says in 1 Corinthians 11:7 that man is the image and glory of God, while women are the glory of man.

9 - The Bible contains lots of contradictions. Why don't we find those contradictions copied in the Quran? For a list of few of the contradictions in the Bible see: http://www.bibleislam.com/bible_contradictions.php

10 - The Quran says that one of Noah's sons was not saved from the flood because he was an unbeliever (Sura 11). Does the Bible say such thing?

11 - The Quran (10:90) tells us that Pharaoh tried to seek forgiveness from God. Does the Bible say the same thing?

12 - Ishmael, the son of Abraham, is considered a Prophet and a Messenger in the Quran. Does the Bible say that "Ishmael is a prophet"?

13 – We read in Surat Al-Nahl in the Quran, that the honey bee produces honey with different hues which is healthy and beneficial for mankind. Just recently, Apitherapy came up with a fantastic cure for arthritist and other chronic diseases–this therapy is called bee sting therapy, where the bee stings the patient and the venom would cure the pain. In addition, the Quran also says that the female bee is responsible for building the hive and collecting the honey. All that is proved by science today. I wonder which book of the Bible says such thing! Search the web for "Bee Sting Therapy" or "Apitherapy" to find out more.

14 - In the 16th verse of Surat Al-'Alaq, we read: {A lying sinful forelock!} Psychologists and neurologists have confirmed that it is in this area of the brain where morals and behavior are processed. Therefore, when someone decides to lie, this decision comes from that front part of the brain, and the Quran refers to that specific part when it refers to lying. Now, I wonder from which Bible passage did Mohammad (s) copy that from.

15 - In the book of Genesis we read the story about what happened to Abraham when he went to Egypt. The Bible tells us that he sold his honor by allowing his wife to become Pharaoh's concubine, so that he could be treated well instead of being killed. Now there is nowhere in the Quran where such accusation is attributed to Prophet Abraham. I wonder why didn't Prophet Mohammad (s) copy such thing from the Bible.

Walhamdulilahi Rabbil Alameen

Believing in prophets is part and parcel of being a Muslim. It is documented in the Quran that belief in all the prophets is obligatory on every Muslim. It specifically says, *"So [you believers], say, 'We believe in God and in what was sent down to us and what was sent down to Abraham, Ishmael, Isaac, Jacob, and the Tribes, and what was given to Moses, Jesus, and all the prophets by their Lord. We make no distinction between any of them, and we devote ourselves to Him."* (2:136)

According to this citation, a Muslim is obligated to accept and revere all of the prophets. The Quran also ties between the belief in the prophets and righteousness to one another. One can't be righteous and reject genuine prophets. An example is, *"Goodness does not consist in turning your face towards East or West. The truly good are those who believe in God and the Last Day, in the angels, the Scripture, and the prophets; who give away some of their wealth, however much they cherish it, to their relatives, to orphans, the needy, travelers and beggars, and to liberate those in bondage; those who keep up the prayer and pay the prescribed alms; who keep pledges whenever they make them; who are steadfast in misfortune, adversity, and times of danger. These are the ones who are true, and it is they who are aware of God."* (2:177)

The Quran indicates very clearly that to deny one prophet means that one is denying all of them: *"As for those who ignore God and His messengers and want to make a distinction between them, saying, 'We believe in some but not in others,' seeking a middle way, they are really disbelievers: We have prepared a humiliating punishment for those who disbelieve."* (4:150-151)

Prophets Mentioned in Quran

Those that are mentioned specifically by name are a total of twenty-five. Eighteen of which appear in four successive verses of the Quran: *"Such was the argument We gave to Abraham against his people – We raise in rank whoever We will – your Lord is all wise, all knowing. We gave him Isaac and Jacob, each of whom We guided, as We had guided Noah before, and among his descendants were David, Solomon, Job, Joseph, Moses, and Aaron – in this way We reward those who do good – Zachariah, John, Jesus, and Elijah – every one of them was righteous – Ishmael, Elisha, Jonah, and Lot. We favored each one of them over other people."* (6:83-86)

In five other places in the Quran the other seven are mentioned. They are Adam, regarded as the first prophet, Hud, Shuaib, Idrees, Thulkifl (believed to be Issaquah) Salleh and finally prophet

Muhammad, may peace and blessings of God be upon them all. A total of twenty-five are mentioned by name in the Qur'an and most of them are familiar to the Judeo Christian faiths.

At the same time, the Quran also indicated that these were not the only prophets that were raised to humanity. Indeed, the Quran says, *"and there never was a people, without a warner having lived among them (in the past)"* **(35:24). The** *warner* **in this context is the same as a prophet. More specifically, God declares in the Quran:** *"to every people (was sent) an apostle."* **(10:47) He goes on to explain,** *"We did aforetime send apostles before thee: of them there are some whose story We have related to thee, and some whose story We have not related to thee."* **(40:78)**

The stories of prophets in the Quran are not there just for historical interest. For those who are familiar with the Bible, it is not just a chronology telling a story as such. The Quran discusses the story and at times omits some minor details while focusing on the lessons that can be learned from studying the history of those prophets.

Prophet Muhammad was the last of all the prophets and messengers of God through whom the entire mission of prophet-hood was brought to its final most comprehensive and complete format.

Biography of Muhammad by a non muslim . By Prof. K. S. Ramakrishna Rao, Head of the Dept. of Philosophy, Govt. College for Women. University of Mysore, Mandya-571401 (Karnatika, India).

Re-printed from "Islam and Modern age", Hydrabad, March 1978.

In the desert of Arabia was Mohammad born, according to Muslim historians, on April 20, 571. The name means highly praised. He is to me the greatest mind among all the sons of Arabia. He means so much more than all the poets and kings that preceded him in that impenetrable desert of red sand.

When he appeared Arabia was a desert — a nothing. Out of nothing a new world was fashioned by the mighty spirit of Mohammad — a new life, a new culture, a new civilization, a new kingdom which extended from Morocco to Indies and influenced the thought and life of three continents — Asia, Africa and Europe.

When I thought of writing on Mohammad the prophet, I was a bit hesitant because it was to write about a religion I do not profess and it is a delicate matter to do so for there are many persons professing various religions and belonging to diverse school of thought and denominations even in same religion. Though it is sometimes, claimed that religion is entirely personal yet it can not be gain-said that it has a tendency to envelop the whole universe seen as well unseen. It somehow permeates something or other our hearts, our souls, our minds their conscious as well as subconscious and unconscious levels too. The problem assumes overwhelming importance when there is a deep conviction that our past, present and future all hang by the soft delicate, tender silked cord. If we further happen to be highly sensitive, the center of gravity is very likely to be always in a state of extreme tension. Looked at from this point of view, the less said about other religion the better. Let our religions be deeply hidden and embedded in the resistance of our innermost hearts fortified by unbroken seals on our lips.

But there is another aspect of this problem. Man lives in society. Our lives are bound with the lives of others willingly or unwillingly, directly or indirectly. We eat the food grown in the same soil, drink water, from the same the same spring and breathe the same air. Even while staunchly holding our own views, it would be helpful, if we try to adjust ourselves to our surroundings, if we also know to some extent, how the mind our neighbor moves and what the main springs of his actions are. From this angle of vision it is highly desirable that one should try to know all religions of the world, in the proper sprit, to promote mutual understanding and better appreciation of our neighborhood, immediate and remote.

Further, our thoughts are not scattered as appear to be on the surface. They have got themselves crystallized around a few nuclei in the form of great world religions and living faiths that guide and motivate the lives of millions that inhabit this earth of ours. It is our duty, in one sense if we have the ideal of ever becoming a citizen of the world before us, to make a little attempt to know the great religions and system of philosophy that have ruled mankind.

In spite of these preliminary remarks, the ground in these field of religion, where there is often a conflict between intellect and emotion is so slippery that one is constantly reminded of fools that rush in where angels fear to tread. It is also not so complex from another point of view. The subject of my writing is about the tenets of a religion which is historic and its prophet who is also a historic personality. Even a hostile critic like Sir William Muir speaking about the holy Quran says that. "There is probably in the world no other book which has remained twelve centuries with so pure text." I may also add Prophet Mohammad is also a historic personality, every event of whose life has been most carefully recorded and even the minutest details preserved intact for the posterity. His life and works are not wrapped in mystery.

My work today is further lightened because those days are fast disappearing when Islam was highly misrepresented by some of its critics for reasons political and otherwise. Prof. Bevan writes in Cambridge Medieval History, "Those account of Mohammad and Islam which were published in Europe before the beginning of 19th century are now to be regarded as literary curiosities." My problem is to write this monograph is easier because we are now generally not fed on this kind of history and much time need be spent on pointing out our misrepresentation of Islam.

The theory of Islam and Sword for instance is not heard now frequently in any quarter worth the name. The principle of Islam that there is no compulsion in religion is well known. Gibbon, a historian of world repute says, "A pernicious tenet has been imputed to Mohammadans, the duty of extirpating all the religions by sword." This charge based on ignorance and bigotry, says the eminent historian, is refuted by Quran, by history of Musalman conquerors and by their public and legal toleration of Christian worship. The great success of Mohammad's life had been effected by sheer moral force, without a stroke of sword.

But in pure self-defense, after repeated efforts of conciliation had utterly failed, circumstances dragged him into the battlefield. But the prophet of Islam changed the whole strategy of the battlefield. The total number of casualties in all the wars that took place during his lifetime when the whole Arabian Peninsula came under his banner, does not exceed a few hundreds in all. But even on the battlefield he taught the Arab barbarians to pray, to pray not individually, but in congregation to God the Almighty. During the dust and storm of warfare whenever the time for prayer came, and it comes five times a every day, the congregation prayer had not to be postponed even on the battlefield. A party had to be engaged in bowing their heads before God while other was engaged with the enemy. After finishing the prayers, the two parties had to exchange their positions. To the Arabs, who would fight for forty years on the slight provocation that a camel belonging to the guest of one tribe had strayed into the grazing land belonging to other tribe and both sides had fought till they lost 70,000 lives in all; threatening the extinction of both the tribes to such furious Arabs, the Prophet of Islam taught self-control and discipline to the extent of praying even on the battlefield. In an aged of barbarism, the Battlefield itself was humanized and strict instructions were issued not to cheat, not to break trust, not to mutilate, not to kill a child or woman or an old man, not to hew down date palm nor burn it, not to cut a fruit tree, not to molest any person engaged in worship. His own treatment with his bitterest enemies is the noblest example for his followers. At the conquest of Mecca, he stood at the zenith of his power. The city which had refused to listen to his mission, which had tortured him and his followers, which had driven him and his people into exile and which had unrelentingly persecuted and boycotted him even when he had taken refuge in a place more than 200 miles away, that city now lay at his feet. By the laws of war he could have justly avenged all the cruelties inflicted on him and his people. But what treatment did he accord to them? Mohammad's heart flowed with affection and he declared, "This day, there is no REPROOF against you and you are all free." "This day" he proclaimed, "I trample under my feet all distinctions between man and man, all hatred between man and man."

This was one of the chief objects why he permitted war in self defense, that is to unite human beings. And when once this object was achieved, even his worst enemies were pardoned. Even those who killed his beloved uncle, Hamazah, mangled his body, ripped it open, even chewed a piece of his liver.

The principles of universal brotherhood and doctrine of the equality of mankind which he proclaimed represents one very great contribution of Mohammad to the social uplift of humanity. All great religions have preached the same doctrine but the prophet of Islam had put this theory into actual practice and its value will be fully recognized, perhaps centuries hence, when international consciousness being awakened, racial prejudices may disappear and greater brotherhood of humanity come into existence.

Miss. Sarojini Naidu speaking about this aspect of Islam says, "It was the first religion that preached and practiced democracy; for in the mosque, when the minaret is sounded and the worshipers are gathered together, the democracy of Islam is embodied five times a day when the peasant and the king kneel side by side and proclaim, God alone is great." The great poetess of India continues, "I have been struck over and over again by this indivisible unity of Islam that makes a man instinctively a brother. When you meet an Egyptian, an Algerian and Indian and a Turk in London, it matters not that Egypt is the motherland of one and India is the motherland of another."

Mahatma Gandhi, in his inimitable style, says "Some one has said that Europeans in South Africa dread the advent Islam — Islam that civilized Spain, Islam that took the torch light to Morocco and preached to the world the Gospel of brotherhood. The Europeans of South Africa dread the Advent of Islam. They may claim equality with the white races. They may well dread it, if brotherhood is a sin. If it is equality of colored races then their dread is well founded."

Every year, during the Haj, the world witnesses the wonderful spectacle of this international Exhibition of Islam in leveling all distinctions of race, color and rank. Not only the Europeans, the African, the Arabian, the Persian, the Indians, the Chinese all meet together in Medina as members of one divine family, but they are clad in one dress every person in two simple pieces of white seamless cloth, one piece round the loin the other piece over the shoulders, bare head without pomp or ceremony, repeating "Here am I O God; at thy command; thou art one and alone; Here am I." Thus there remains nothing to differentiate the high from the low and every pilgrim carries home the impression of the international significance of Islam.

In the opinion of Prof. Hurgronje "the league of nations founded by prophet of Islam put the principle of international unity of human brotherhood on such Universal foundations as to show candle to other nations." In the words of same Professor "the fact is that no nation of the world can show a parallel to what Islam has done the realization of the idea of the League of Nations."

The prophet of Islam brought the reign of democracy in its best form. The Caliph Caliph Ali and the son in-law of the prophet, the Caliph Mansur, Abbas, the son of Caliph Mamun and many other caliphs and kings had to appear before the judge as ordinary men in Islamic courts. Even today we all know how the black Negroes were treated by the civilized white races. Consider the state of BILAL, a Negro Slave, in the days of the prophet of Islam nearly 14 centuries ago. The office of calling Muslims to prayer was considered to be of status in the early days of Islam and it was offered to this Negro slave. After the conquest of Mecca, the Prophet ordered him to call for prayer and the Negro slave, with his black color and his thick lips, stood over the roof of the holy mosque at Mecca called the Ka'ba the most historic and the holiest mosque in the Islamic world, when some proud Arabs painfully cried loud, "Oh, this black Negro Slave, woe be to him. He stands on the roof of holy Ka'ba to call for prayer." At that moment, the prophet announced to the world, this verse of the holy QURAN for the first time.
"O mankind, surely we have created you, families and tribes, so you may know one another. Surely, the most honorable of you with God is MOST RIGHTEOUS AMONG you. Surely, God is Knowing, Aware."

And these words of the holy Quran created such a mighty transformation that the Caliph of Islam, the purest of Arabs by birth, offered their daughter in marriage to this Negro Slave, and whenever, the second Caliph of Islam, known to history as Umar the great, the commander of faithful, saw this Negro slave, he immediately stood in reverence and welcomed him by "Here come our master; Here come our lord." What a tremendous change was brought by Quran in the Arabs, the proudest people at that time on the earth. This is the reason why Goethe, the greatest of German poets, speaking about the Holy Quran declared that, "This book will go on exercising through all ages a most potent influence." This is also the reason why George Bernard Shaw says, "If any religion has a chance or ruling over England, say, Europe, within the next 100 years, it is Islam".

It is this same democratic spirit of Islam that emancipated women from the bondage of man. Sir Charles Edward Archibald Hamilton says "Islam teaches the inherent sinlessness of man. It teaches that man and woman and woman have come from the same essence, posses the same soul and have been equipped with equal capabilities for intellectual, spiritual and moral attainments."

The Arabs had a very strong tradition that one who can smite with the spear and can wield the sword would inherit. But Islam came as the defender of the weaker sex and entitled women to share the inheritance of their parents. It gave women, centuries ago right of owning property, yet it was only 12 centuries later, in 1881, that England, supposed to be the cradle of democracy adopted this institution of Islam and the act was called "the married woman act", but centuries earlier, the Prophet of Islam had proclaimed that "Woman are twin halves of men. The rights of women are sacred. See that women maintained rights granted to them."

Islam is not directly concerned with political and economic systems, but indirectly and in so far as political and economic affairs influence man's conduct, it does lay down some very important principles to govern economic life. According to Prof. Massignon, it maintains the balance between exaggerated opposites and has always in view the building of character which is the basis of civilization. This is secured by its law of inheritance, by an organized system of charity known as Zakat, and by regarding as illegal all anti-social practices in the economic field like monopoly, usury, securing of predetermined unearned income and increments, cornering markets, creating monopolies, creating an artificial scarcity of any commodity in order to force the prices to rise. Gambling is illegal. Contribution to schools, to places of worship, hospitals, digging of wells, opening of orphanages are highest acts of virtue. Orphanages have sprung for the first time, it is said, under the teaching of the prophet of Islam. The world owes its orphanages to this prophet born an orphan. "Good all this" says Carlyle about Mohammad. "The natural voice of humanity, of pity and equity, dwelling in the heart of this wild son of nature, speaks."

A historian once said a great man should be judged by three tests: Was he found to be of true metel by his contemporaries? Was he great enough to raise above the standards of his age? Did he leave anything as permanent legacy to the world at large? This list may be further extended but all these three tests of greatness are eminently satisfied to the highest degree in case of prophet Mohammad. Some illustrations of the last two have already been mentioned.

The first is: Was the Prophet of Islam found to be of true metel by his contemporaries?

Historical records show that all the contemporaries of Mohammad both friends foes, acknowledged the sterling qualities, the spotless honesty, the noble virtues, the absolute sincerity and every trustworthiness of the apostle of Islam in all walks of life and in every sphere of human activity. Even the Jews and those who did not believe in his message, adopted him as the arbiter in their personal disputes by virtue of his perfect impartiality. Even those who did not believe in his message were forced to say "O Mohammad, we do not call you a liar, but we deny him who has given you a book and inspired you with a message." They thought he was one possessed. They tried violence to cure him. But the best of them saw that a new light had dawned on him and they hastened him to seek the enlightenment. It is a notable feature in the history of prophet of Islam that his nearest relation, his beloved cousin and his bosom friends, who know him most intimately, were not thoroughly imbued with the truth of his mission and were convinced of the genuineness of his divine inspiration. If these men and women, noble, intelligent, educated and intimately acquainted with his private life had perceived the slightest signs of deception, fraud, earthliness, or lack of faith in him, Mohammad's moral hope of regeneration, spiritual awakening, and social reform would all have been foredoomed to a failure and whole edifice would have crumbled to pieces in a moment. On the contrary, we find that devotion of his followers was such that he was voluntarily acknowledged as dictator of their lives. They braved for him persecutions and danger; they trusted, obeyed and honored him even in the most excruciating torture and severest mental agony caused by excommunication even unto death. Would this have been so, had they noticed the slightest backsliding in their master?

Read the history of the early converts to Islam, and every heart would melt at the sight of the brutal treatment of innocent Muslim men and women.

Sumayya, an innocent women, is cruelly torn into pieces with spears. An example is made of "Yassir whose legs are tied to two camels and the beast were are driven in opposite directions", Khabbab bin Arth is made lie down on the bed of burning coal with the brutal legs of their merciless tyrant on his breast so that he may not move and this makes even the fat beneath his skin melt. "Khabban bin Adi is put to death in a cruel manner by mutilation and cutting off his flesh piece-meal." In the midst of his tortures, being asked weather he did not wish Mohammad in his place while he was in his house with his family, the sufferer cried out that he was gladly prepared to sacrifice himself his family and children and why was it that these sons and daughters of Islam not only surrendered to their prophet their allegiance but also made a gift of their hearts and souls to their master? Is not the intense faith and conviction on part of immediate followers of Mohammad, the noblest testimony to his sincerity and to his utter self-absorption in his appointed task?

And these men were not of low station or inferior mental caliber. Around him in quite early days, gathered what was best and noblest in Mecca, its flower and cream, men of position, rank, wealth and culture, and from his own kith and kin, those who knew all about his life. All the first four Caliphs, with their towering personalities, were converts of this period.

The Encyclopedia Brittanica says that "Mohammad is the most successful of all Prophets and religious personalities".

But the success was not the result of mere accident. It was not a hit of fortune. It was a recognition of fact that he was found to be true metal by his contemporaries. It was the result of his admirable and all compelling personality.

The personality of Mohammad! It is most difficult to get into the truth of it. Only a glimpse of it I can catch. What a dramatic succession of picturesque scenes. There is Mohammad the Prophet, there is Mohammad the General; Mohammad the King; Mohammad the Warrior; Mohammad the Businessman; Mohammad the Preacher; Mohammad the Philosopher; Mohammad the Statesman; Mohammad the Orator; Mohammad the reformer; Mohammad the Refuge of orphans; Mohammad the Protector of slaves; Mohammad the Emancipator of women; Mohammad the Law-giver; Mohammad the Judge; Mohammad the Saint.

And in all these magnificent roles, in all these departments of human activities, he is like, a hero..

Orphanhood is extreme of helplessness and his life upon this earth began with it; Kingship is the height of the material power and it ended with it. From an orphan boy to a persecuted refugee and then to an overlord, spiritual as well as temporal, of a whole nation and Arbiter of its destinies, with all its trials and temptations, with all its vicissitudes and changes, its lights and shades, its up and downs, its terror and splendor, he has stood the fire of the world and came out unscathed to serve as a model in every face of life. His achievements are not limited to one aspect of life, but cover the whole field of human conditions.

If for instance, greatness consist in the purification of a nation, steeped in barbarism and immersed in absolute moral darkness, that dynamic personality who has transformed, refined and uplifted an entire nation, sunk low as the Arabs were, and made them the torch-bearer of civilization and learning, has every claim to greatness. If greatness lies in unifying the discordant elements of society by ties of brotherhood and charity, the prophet of the desert has got every title to this distinction. If greatness consists in reforming those warped in degrading and blind superstition and pernicious practices of every kind, the prophet of Islam has wiped out superstitions and irrational fear from the hearts of millions. If it lies in displaying high morals, Mohammad has been admitted by friend and foe as Al Amin, or the faithful. If a conqueror is a great man, here is a person who rose from helpless orphan and an humble creature to be the ruler of Arabia, the equal to Chosroes and Caesars, one who founded great empire that has survived all these 14 centuries. If the devotion that a leader commands is the criterion of greatness, the prophet's name even today exerts a magic charm over millions of souls, spread all over the world.

He had not studied philosophy in the school of Athens of Rome, Persia, India, or China. Yet, He could proclaim the highest truths of eternal value to mankind. Illiterate himself, he could yet speak with an eloquence and fervor which moved men to tears, to tears of ecstasy. Born an orphan blessed with no worldly goods, he was loved by all. He had studied at no military academy; yet he could organize his forces against tremendous odds and gained victories through the moral forces which he marshaled. Gifted men with genius for preaching are rare. Descartes included the perfect preacher among the rarest kind in the world. Hitler in his Mein Kamp has expressed a similar view. He says "A great theorist is seldom a great leader. An Agitator is more likely to posses these qualities. He will always be a great leader. For leadership means ability to move masses of men. The talents to produce ideas has nothing in common with capacity for leadership." "But", he says, "The Union of theorists, organizer and leader in one man, is the rarest phenomenon on this earth; Therein consists greatness."

In the person of the Prophet of Islam the world has seen this rarest phenomenon walking on the earth, walking in flesh and blood.

And more wonderful still is what the reverend Bosworth Smith remarks, "Head of the state as well as the Church, he was Caesar and Pope in one; but, he was pope without the pope's claims, and Caesar without the legions of Caesar, without an standing army, without a bodyguard, without a palace, without a fixed revenue. If ever any man had the right to say that he ruled by a right divine It was Mohammad, for he had all the power without instruments and without its support. He cared not for dressing of power. The simplicity of his private life was in keeping with his public life."

After the fall of Mecca, more than one million square miles of land lay at his feet, Lord of Arabia, he mended his own shoes and coarse woolen garments, milked the goats, swept the hearth, kindled the fire and attended the other menial offices of the family. The entire town of Medina where he lived grew wealthy in the later days of his life. Everywhere there was gold and silver in plenty and yet in those days of prosperity many weeks would elapse without a fire being kindled in the hearth of the king of Arabia, His food being dates and water. His family would go hungry many nights successively because they could not get anything to eat in the evening. He slept on no soften bed but on a palm mat, after a long busy day to spend most of his night in prayer, often bursting with tears before his creator to grant him strength to discharge his duties. As the reports go, his voice would get choked with weeping and it would appear as if a cooking pot was on fire and boiling had commenced. On the very day of his death his only assets were few coins a part of which went to satisfy a debt and rest was given to a needy person who came to his house for charity. The clothes in which he breathed his last had many patches. The house from where light had spread to the world was in darkness because there was no oil in the lamp.

Circumstances changed, but the prophet of God did not. In victory or in defeat, in power or in adversity, in affluence or in indigence, he is the same man, disclosed the same character. Like all the ways and laws of God, Prophets of God are unchangeable.

An honest man, as the saying goes, is the noblest work of God, Mohammad was more than honest. He was human to the marrow of his bones. Human sympathy, human love was the music of his soul. To serve man, to elevate man, to purify man, to educate man, in a word to humanize man-this was the object of his mission, the be-all and end all of his life. In thought, in word, in action he had the good of humanity as his sole inspiration, his sole guiding principle.

He was most unostentatious and selfless to the core. What were the titles he assumed? Only true servant of God and His Messenger. Servant first, and then a messenger. A Messenger and prophet like many other prophets in every part of the world, some known to you, many not known you. If one does not believe in any of these truths one ceases to be a Muslim. It is an article of faith.

"Looking at the circumstances of the time and unbounded reverence of his followers" says a western writer "the most miraculous thing about Mohammad is, that he never claimed the power of working miracles." Miracles were performed but not to propagate his faith and were attributed entirely to God and his inscrutable ways. He would plainly say that he was a man like others. He had no treasures of earth or heaven. Nor did he claim to know the secrets of that lie in womb of future. All this was in an age when miracles were supposed to be ordinary occurrences, at the back and call of the commonest saint, when the whole atmosphere was surcharged with supernaturalism in Arabia and outside Arabia.

He turned the attention of his followers towards the study of nature and its laws, to understand them and appreciate the Glory of God. The Quran says,

"God did not create the heavens and the earth and all that is between them in play. He did not create them all but with the truth. But most men do not know."

The world is not illusion, nor without purpose. It has been created with the truth. The number of verses inviting close observation of nature are several times more than those that relate to prayer, fasting, pilgrimage etc. all put together. The Muslim under its influence began to observe nature closely and this give birth to the scientific spirit of the observation and experiment which was unknown to the Greeks. While the Muslim Botanist Ibn Baitar wrote on Botany after collecting plants from all parts of the world, described by Myer in his Gesch. der Botanikaa-s, a monument of industry, while Al Byruni traveled for forty years to collect mineralogical specimens, and Muslim Astronomers made some observations extending even over twelve years. Aristotle wrote on Physics without performing a single experiment, wrote on natural history, carelessly stating without taking the trouble to ascertain the most verifiable fact that men have more teeth than animal. Galen, the greatest authority on classical anatomy informed that the lower jaw consists of two bones, a statement which is accepted unchallenged for centuries till Abdul Lateef takes the trouble to examine a human skeleton. After enumerating several such instances, Robert Priffault concludes in his well known book The making of humanity, "The debt of our science to the Arabs does not consist in starting discovers or revolutionary theories. Science owes a great more to Arabs culture; it owes is existence." The same writer says "The Greeks systematized, generalized and theorized but patient ways of investigation, the accumulation of positive knowledge, the minute methods of science, detailed and prolonged observation, experimental inquiry, were altogether alien to Greek temperament. What we call science arose in Europe as result of new methods of investigation, of the method of experiment, observation, measurement, of the development of Mathematics in form unknown to the Greeks. That spirit and these methods, concludes the same author, were introduced into the European world by Arabs."

It is the same practical character of the teaching of Prophet Mohammad that gave birth to the scientific spirit, that has also sanctified the daily labors and the so called mundane affairs. The Quran says that God has created man to worship him but the word worship has a connotation of its own. Gods worship is not confined to prayer alone, but every act that is done with the purpose of winning approval of God and is for the benefit of the humanity comes under its purview. Islam sanctifies life and all its pursuits provided they are performed with honesty, justice and pure intents. It obliterates the age-long distinction between the sacred and profane. The Quran says if you eat clean things and thank God for it, it is an act of worship. It is saying of the prophet of Islam that Morsel of food that one places in the mouth of his wife is an act of virtue to be rewarded by God. Another tradition of the Prophet says "He who is satisfying the desire of his heart will be rewarded by God provided the methods adopted are permissible." A person was listening to him exclaimed 'O Prophet of God, he is answering the calls of passions, is only satisfying the craving of his heart. Forthwith came the reply, "Had he adopted an awful method for the satisfaction of his urge, he would have been punished; then why should he not be rewarded for following the right course."

This new conception of religion that it should also devote itself to the betterment of this life rather than concern itself exclusively with super mundane affairs, has led to a new orientation of moral values. Its abiding influence on the common relations of mankind in the affairs of every day life, its deep power over the masses, its regulation of their conception of rights and duty, its suitability and adaptability to the ignorant savage and the wise philosopher are characteristic features of the teaching of the Prophet of Islam.

But it should be most carefully born in mind this stress on good actions is not the sacrifice correctness of faith. While there are various school of thought, one praising faith at the expense of deeds, another exhausting various acts to the detriment of correct belief, Islam is based on correct faith and righteous actions. Means are important as the end and ends are as important as the means. It is an organic Unity. Together they live and thrive. Separate them and both decay and die. In Islam faith can not be divorced from the action. Right knowledge should be transferred into right action to produce the right results. How often the words came in Quran — Those who believe and do good thing, they alone shall enter paradise. Again and again, not less than fifty times these words are repeated as if too much stress can not be laid on them. Contemplation is encouraged but mere contemplation is not the goal. Those who believe and do nothing can not exist in Islam. These who believe and do wrong are inconceivable. Divine law is the law of effort and not of ideals. It chalks out for the men the path of eternal progress from knowledge to action and from action to satisfaction.

But what is the correct faith from which right action spontaneously proceeds resulting in complete satisfaction. Here the central doctrine of Islam is the Unity of God. There is no God but God is the pivot from which hangs the whole teaching and practice of Islam. He is unique not only as regards his divine being but also as regards his divine attributes.

As regards the attributes of God, Islam adopts here as in other things too, the law of golden mean. It avoids on the one hand, the view of God which divests the divine being of every attribute and rejects, on the other, the view which likens him to things material. The Quran says, On the one hand, there is nothing which is like him, on the other, it affirms that he is Seeing, Hearing, Knowing. He is the King who is without a stain of fault or deficiency, the mighty ship of His power floats upon the ocean of justice and equity. He is the Beneficent, the Merciful. He is the Guardian over all. Islam does not stop with this positive statement. It adds further which is its most special characteristic, the negative aspects of problem. There is also no one else who is guardian over everything. He is the meander of every breakage, and no one else is the meander of any breakage. He is the restorer of every loss and no one else is the restorer of any loss what-so-over. There is no God but one God, above any need, the maker of bodies, creator of souls, the Lord of the day of judgment, and in short, in the words of Quran, to him belong all excellent qualities.

Regarding the position of man in relation to the Universe, the Quran says:

"God has made subservient to you whatever is on the earth or in universe. You are destined to rule over the Universe."

But in relation to God, the Quran says:

"O man God has bestowed on you excellent faculties and has created life and death to put you to test in order to see whose actions are good and who has deviated from the right path."

In spite of free will which he enjoys, to some extent, every man is born under certain circumstances and continues to live under certain circumstances beyond his control. With regard to this God says, according to Islam, it is my will to create any man under condition that seem best to me. cosmic plans finite mortals can not fully comprehend. But I will certainly test you in prosperity as well in adversity, in health as well as in sickness, in heights as well as in depths. My ways of testing differ from man to man, from hour to hour. In adversity do not despair and do resort to unlawful means. It is but a passing phase. In prosperity do not forget God. God-gifts are given only as trusts. You are always on trial, every moment on test. In this sphere of life there is not to reason why, there is but to do and die. If you live in accordance with God; and if you die, die in the path of God. You may call it fatalism. but this type of fatalism is a condition of vigorous increasing effort, keeping you ever on the alert. Do not consider this temporal life on earth as the end of human existence. There is a life after death and it is eternal. Life after death is only a connection link, a door that opens up hidden reality of life. Every action in life however insignificant, produces a lasting effect. It is correctly recorded somehow. Some of the ways of God are known to you, but many of his ways are hidden from you. What is hidden in you and from you in this world will be unrolled and laid open before you in the next. the virtuous will enjoy the blessing of God which the eye has not seen, nor has the ear heard, nor has it entered into the hearts of men to conceive of they will march onward reaching higher and higher stages of evolution. Those who have wasted opportunity in this life shall under the inevitable law, which makes every man taste of what he has done, be subjugated to a course of treatment of the spiritual diseases which they have brought about with their own hands. Beware, it is terrible ordeal. Bodily pain is torture, you can bear somehow. Spiritual pain is hell, you will find it almost unbearable. Fight in this life itself the tendencies of the spirit prone to evil, tempting to lead you into iniquities ways. Reach the next stage when the self-accusing sprit in your conscience is awakened and the soul is anxious to attain moral excellence and revolt against disobedience. This will lead you to the final stage of the soul at rest, contented with God, finding its happiness and delight in him alone. The soul no more stumbles. The stage of struggle passes away. Truth is victorious and falsehood lays down its arms. All complexes will then be resolved. Your house will not be divided against itself. Your personality will get integrated round the central core of submission to the will of God and complete surrender to his divine purpose. All hidden energies will then be released. The soul then will have peace. God will then address you:

"O thou soul that art at rest, and restest fully contented with thy Lord return to thy Lord. He pleased with thee and thou pleased with him; So enter among my servants and enter into my paradise."

This is the final goal for man; to become, on the, one hand, the master of the universe and on the other, to see that his soul finds rest in his Lord, that not only his Lord will be pleased with him but that he is also pleased with his Lord. Contentment, complete contentment, satisfaction, complete satisfaction, peace, complete peace. The love of God is his food at this stage and he drinks deep at the fountain of life. Sorrow and defeat do not overwhelm him and success does not find him in vain and exulting.

The western nations are only trying to become the master of the Universe. But their souls have not found peace and rest.

Thomas Carlyle, struck by this philosophy of life writes "and then also Islam-that we must submit to God; that our whole strength lies in resigned submission to Him, whatsoever he does to us, the thing he sends to us, even if death and worse than death, shall be good, shall be best; we resign ourselves to God." The same author continues "If this be Islam, says Goethe, do we not all live in Islam?" Carlyle himself answers this question of Goethe and says "Yes, all of us that have any moral life, we all live so. This is yet the highest wisdom that heaven has revealed to our earth."

Jesus in islam & quran

"And mention in the Book (the Quran), Mary, when she withdrew in seclusion from her family to a place facing east. She placed a screen (to screen herself) from them; then We sent to her a spirit from Us, (the angel Gabriel), and he appeared before her in the form of a man in all respects. She said: 'Verily, I seek refuge with the Most Gracious (God) from you, if you do fear God.' (The angel) said: 'I am only a messenger from your Lord, (to announce) to you the gift of a righteous son.' She said: 'How can I have a son, when no man hath touched me, nor am I unchaste?' He said: 'So (it will be), your Lord said That is easy for Me (God): And (We wish) to appoint him as a sign to mankind and a mercy from Us (God), and it is a matter (already) decreed (by God).'" (Quran 19:16-21)

"Indeed, the likeness of Jesus with God is as the likeness of Adam. He created him of dust, then He said to him: 'Be!' and he was.'" (Quran 3:59)

Muslims, like Christians believe that Jesus performed miracles. These miracles were performed by the will and permission of God, Who has power and control over all things.

"Then will God say: 'O Jesus the son of Mary! Recount My favor to you and to your mother. Behold! I strengthened you with the Holy Spirit (the angel Gabriel) so that you did speak to the people in childhood and in maturity. Behold! I taught you the Book and Wisdom, the Torah and the Gospel. And behold: you make out of clay, as it were, the figure of a bird, by My leave, and you breathe into it, and it becomes a bird by My leave, and you heal those born blind, and the lepers by My leave. And behold! You bring forth the dead by My leave. And behold! I did restrain the Children of Israel from (violence to you) when you did show them the Clear Signs, and the unbelievers among them said: 'This is nothing but evident magic.'" (Quran 5:110)

God sent all prophets with miracles specific to the nation to whom they were sent to prove the veracity of their message. These miracles were not performed of their own accord; rather, they were only manifest in their hands by God's will. The miracles performed by Jesus were no different. The Jews were well advanced in the field of medicine, and the miracles which Jesus brought were of this nature, proving the truth of His message and in order to convince the Jews.

> "They have certainly disbelieved who say, 'God is the Messiah, the son of Mary' while the Messiah has said, 'O Children of Israel, worship God, my Lord and your Lord...'" (Quran 5:72)

God says about the belief that Jesus is part of a "Trinity":

> "They have certainly disbelieved who say, 'God is the third of three.' (Rather) there is none worthy of worship except One (God). And if they do not desist from what they are saying, there will surely afflict the disbelievers among them a painful punishment. So will they not repent to God and seek His forgiveness? And God is Forgiving and Merciful. The Messiah (Jesus), son of Mary, was no more than a Messenger before whom many Messengers have passed away; and his mother adhered wholly to truthfulness, and they both ate food (as other mortals do). See how We make Our signs clear to them; and see where they are turning away!" (Quran 5:73-75)

And also: "O People of the Book (Jews and Christians)! Do not exceed the limits in your religion, and attribute to God nothing except the truth. The Messiah, Jesus, son of Mary, was only a Messenger of God, and His command that He conveyed unto Mary, and a spirit from Him. So believe in God and in His Messengers, and do not say: 'God is a Trinity.' Give up this assertion; it would be better for you. For God is indeed (the only) One God. Far be it from His glory that He should have a son. To Him belongs all that is in the heavens and in the earth. And God is sufficient for a guardian." (Quran 4:171)

God deems this belief as an enormity against His Essence:

> "And they say: 'The Most Merciful (God) has taken (for Himself) a son.' Assuredly you utter a hideous thing, whereby almost the heavens are torn, and the earth is split asunder and the mountains fall in ruins; That they ascribe unto the Most Merciful a son, when it is not suitable for (the Majesty of) the Most Merciful that He should take a son. There is none in the heavens and the earth but comes unto the Most Merciful as a slave." (Quran 19:88-93)

On the Day of Judgment, Jesus again will free himself from this false attribution. God gives us a glimpse of what he will say when he is asked about why people

worshipped him:

> "And (beware the Day) when God will say, "O Jesus, Son of Mary, did you say to the people, 'Take me and my mother as deities besides God?'" He will say, 'Exalted are You! It was not for me to say that to which I have no right. If I had said it, You would have known it. You know what is within myself, and I do not know what is within Yourself. Indeed, it is You who is Knower of the unseen. I said not to them except what you commanded me – to worship God, my Lord and your Lord…'" (Quran 5:116-117)

"I am the Lord thy God, which have brought thee out of the land of Egypt, out of the house of bondage. Thou shalt have no other gods before me." (Exodus 20:1-3)

Ascribing a son to God is in clear opposition to that principle for which He created the Creation and sent prophets. God says in the Quran:

"And I did not create the jinn and mankind except to worship Me." (Quran 51:56)

He also said:

"And We certainly sent into every nation a messenger, (saying), 'Worship God and avoid all false objects of worship...'" (Quran 16:36)

"And (remember) when Jesus, son of Mary, said: 'O Children of Israel, I am the Messenger of God sent to you, confirming the Torah (which came) before me...'" (Quran 61:6)

Matthew 5:17-18, Jesus stated:

"Think not that I have come to abolish the law and the (way of) the prophets; I have come not to abolish them but to fulfill them."

another prophet to come after him. God says:

"And when Jesus, son of Mary, said: 'O Children of Israel! Indeed I am the messenger of God unto you, confirming that which was (revealed) before me in the Torah, and bringing good tidings of a messenger who will come after me, whose name is the Praised One.'" (Quran 61:6)

John 14:16-17: "And I will give you another Counselor to be with you forever, even the Spirit of Truth."

It was told by jesus so its none other then prophet Mohammad

Crucifixion

"...They did not kill him, nor did they crucify him, but (another) was made to resemble him to them..." (Quran 4:157)

"God lifted him up to His presence. God is Almighty, All-Wise."

(Quran 4:158) "No bearer of burdens shall bear the burden of another." (Quran 39:7)

"There is not one of the People of the Scripture but will believe in him (Jesus) before his death, and on the Day of Resurrection he will be a witness against them." (Quran 4: 159)

SURAT AL IKHLAS (MAKKAH)
1) Say he is Allah one & only
(2) Allah, the eternal, absolute
3) He begets not, nor is he begotten
(4) And there is none like unto him (Al-Quran)
Some References :
1) www.peacetv.tv   7) www.guideus.tv 8) www.whyislam.org

2) www.islamtomorrow.com
3) www.irf.net
4) Search in Google for free Quran.

PROPHET MUHAMMAD (pbuh) IN THE BIBLE
by Dr. Zakir Naik

Prophet Muhammad (pbuh) in the Old Testament:

The Qur'an mentions in Surah Al-Araf chapter 7 verse 157:

"Those who follow the Messenger, the unlettered Prophet, whom they find mentioned in their own (scriptures) in the law and the Gospel".

1. MUHAMMAD (PBUH) PROPHESISED IN THE BOOK OF DEUTERONOMY:

Almighty God speaks to Moses in Book of Deuteronomy chapter 18 verse 18:

"I will raise them up a Prophet from among their brethren, like unto thee, and I will put my words in his mouth; and he shall speak unto them all that I shall command him."

The Christians say that this prophecy refers to Jesus (pbuh) because Jesus (pbuh) was like Moses (pbuh). Moses (pbuh) was a Jew, as well as Jesus (pbuh) was a Jew. Moses (pbuh) was a Prophet and Jesus (pbuh) was also a Prophet
If these two are the only criteria for this prophecy to be fulfilled, then all the Prophets of the Bible who came after
Moses (pbuh) such as Solomon, Isaiah, Ezekiel, Daniel, Hosea, Joel, Malachi, John the Baptist, etc. (pbut) will
fulfill this prophecy since all were Jews as well as prophets.

However, it is Prophet Muhammad (pbuh) who is like Moses (pbuh):

i) Both had a father and a mother, while Jesus (pbuh) was born miraculously without any male intervention.

[Mathew 1:18 and Luke 1:35 and also Al-Qur'an 3:42-47]

ii) Both were married and had children. Jesus (pbuh) according to the Bible did not marry nor had children.

iii) Both died natural deaths. Jesus (pbuh) has been raised up alive. (4:157-158)

Muhammad (pbuh) is from among the brethren of Moses (pbuh). Arabs are brethren of Jews. Abraham (pbuh) had two sons: Ishmail and Isaac (pbut). The Arabs are the descendants of Ishmail (pbuh) and the Jews are the descendants of Isaac (pbuh).

Words in the mouth:

Prophet Muhammad (pbuh) was unlettered and whatever revelations he received

from Almighty God he repeated them verbatim.

"I will raise them up a Prophet from among their brethren, like unto thee, and will put my words in his mouth; and he shall speak unto them all that I shall command him."

[Deuteronomy 18:18]

iv) Both besides being Prophets were also kings i.e. they could inflict capital punishment. Jesus (pbuh) said, "My kingdom is not of this world." (John 18:36).

v) Both were accepted as Prophets by their people in their lifetime but Jesus (pbuh) was rejected by his
people. John chapter 1 verse 11 states, "He came unto his own, but his own received him not."

iv) Both brought new laws and new regulations for their people. Jesus (pbuh) according to the Bible did not bring any new laws. (Mathew 5:17-18).

112. Surah Al-Ikhlaas or At-Tauhid (The Purity)

1. Say (O Muhammad ( )): "He is Allah, (the) One.

2. "*Allah-us-Samad* (The Self-Sufficient Master, Whom all creatures need, He neither eats nor drinks).

3. "He begets not, nor was He begotten;

4. "And there is none co-equal or comparable unto Him." Quran

(according to historians original bible does not exist) search in google!!!

(The punishment of raping a women in islam is death penalty)!!!

if anyone killed a person not in retaliation of murder, or (and) to spread mischief in the land - it would be as if he killed all mankind, and if anyone saved a life, it would be as if he saved the life of all mankind.Quran.

2. **It is Mentioned in the book of Deuteronomy chapter 18:19**

   "And it shall come to pass, that whosoever will not harken unto my words which he shall speak in my name, I will   require it of him."

3. **Muhammad (pbuh) is prophesised in the book of Isaiah:**

   It is mentioned in the book of Isaiah chapter 29 verse 12:

   "And the book is delivered to him that is not learned, saying, Read this, I pray thee: and he saith, I am not learned."

   When Archangel Gabrail commanded Muhammad (pbuh) by saying Iqra - "Read", he replied, "I am not learned".

4. **prophet Muhammad (pbuh) mentioned by name in the old testament:**

   Prophet Muhammad (pbuh) is mentioned by name in the Song of Solomon chapter 5 verse 16:

   prophet Muhammad (pbuh) mentioned by name in the old testament: Prophet Muhammad (pbuh) is mentioned by name in the Song of Solomon chapter 5 verse 16:"Hikko Mamittakim we kullo Muhammadim Zehdoodeh wa Zehraee Bayna Jerusalem.""His mouth is most sweet: yea, he is altogether lovely. This is my beloved, and this is my friend, O daughters of Jerusalem."In the Hebrew language im is added for respect. Similarely im is added after the name of Prophet Muhammad   (pbuh) to make it Muhammadim. In English translation they have even translated the name of Prophet Muhammad   (pbuh) as "altogether lovely", but in the Old Testament in Hebrew, the name of Prophet Muhammad (pbuh) is yet present.It's majestic plural noun like Elohim which refers to 1 God only.so Muhammadim also refers to 1 Muhammad even though im can refer also to be plural.(Edited by Faisal)

Prophet Muhammad (pbuh) in the New Testament:

Al-Qur'an Chapter 61 Verse 6:

"And remember, Jesus, the son of Mary, said, 'O Children of Israel! I am the messenger of Allah (sent) to you, confirming the Law (which came) before me and giving glad tidings of a messenger to come after me, whose name shall be Ahmed.' But when he came to them with clear signs, they said, 'This is evident sorcery!' "

All the prophecies mentioned in the Old Testament regarding Muhammad (pbuh) besides applying to the Jews also hold good for the Christians.

1. **John chapter 14 verse 16:**

    "And I will pray the Father, and he shall give you another Comforter, that he may abide with you forever."

2. **Gospel of John chapter 15 verse 26:**

    "But when the Comforter is come, whom I will send unto you from the Father, even the Spirit

    of truth, which
    proceedeth from the Father, he shall testify of me."

3. **Gospel of John chapter 16 verse 7:**

    "Nevertheless I tell you the truth; it is expedient for you that I go away: for if I go not away, the Comforter will not
    come unto you; but if I depart, I will send him unto you".

    "Ahmed" or "Muhammad" meaning "the one who praises" or "the praised one" is almost the translation of the
    Greek word *Periclytos*. In the Gospel of John 14:16, 15:26, and 16:7. The word 'Comforter' is used in the English translation for the Greek word *Paracletos* which means advocate or a kind friend rather than a comforter.
    Paracletos is the warped reading for *Periclytos*. Jesus (pbuh) actually prophesised Ahmed by name. Even the
    Greek word *Paraclete* refers to the Prophet (pbuh) who is a mercy for all creatures.

    Some Christians say that the Comforter mentioned in these prophecies refers to the Holy Sprit. They fail to realise
    that the prophecy clearly says that only if Jesus (pbuh) departs will the Comforter

come. The Bible states that the
Holy Spirit was already present on earth before and during the time of Jesus (pbuh), in the womb of Elizabeth, and again when Jesus (pbuh) was being baptised, etc. Hence this prophecy refers to none other than Prophet
Muhammad (pbuh).

4.   **Gospel of John chapter 16 verse 12-14:**

"I have yet many things to say unto you, but ye cannot bear them now. Howbeit when he, the Spirit of truth is come, he will guide you unto all truth: for he shall not speak of himself; but whatsoever he shall hear, that shall he speak: and he will shew you things to come. He shall glorify me".

The Sprit of Truth, spoken about in this prophecy referes to none other than Prophet Muhammad (pbuh)

NOTE: All quotations of the Bible are taken from the King James Version.

Some hadiths (teachings of prophet Muhammad)(pbuh)

Aisha reported: I heard the Messenger of Allah, peace and blessings be upon him, say, "**Gabriel continued to advise me to treat neighbors well until I thought he would make them my heirs.**"Source: Sahih Muslim 2624 Grade: *Sahih* (authentic) according to Imam Muslim

Abu Musa reported: The Prophet, peace and blessings be upon him, said, "The honest Muslim trustee who carries out the orders of those who trusted him and who pays in full with a good heart to the right person is regarded as one of the two who gave charity." Source: Sahih Bukhari 1371, Sahih Muslim [...] Abu Huraira reported: The Messenger of Allah, peace and blessings be upon him, said, "**There is no justification for envy except in two cases. First, a man whom Allah has given the Quran and he recites it during the night and day, so someone says: If I were to be given like this, I would do as he is doing. And second, a man whom Allah has given wealth and he spends it in justice, so someone says: If I were to be given like this, I would do as he is doing.**" Source: Sahih Bukhari 6805 Grade: *Sahih* (authentic) according to Al-Bukhari

Hadith on Zakat: The command to give 2.5% of surplus wealth as alms and charity

Abu Amina Elias | April 5, 2013 Ali ibn Abu Talib reported: The Prophet, peace and blessings be upon him, said, "**If you have two hundred coins and a year has passed, then five coins is due for alms; and you will owe nothing until you own twenty coins, but when you own twenty coins and a year has passed, then half of a coin is due for alms and whatever exceeds that should be calculated likewise.**"Source: Sunan Abu Dawud 1572Grade: *Hasan* (fair) according to Abu Dawud (due to his silence) Abu Dharr reported: My dear friend the Prophet, peace and blessings be upon him, enjoined upon me three deeds, "**Listen to and obey the ruler even if a slave is appointed over you. When you make soup, put some extra water in it and look to the**

people in the neighboring house and give them a reasonable portion of it, and pray your prayers on time, for if you find the Imam praying then pray with him and your prayer will be safeguarded, otherwise it will be voluntary for you."Source: Musnad Ahmad 20918 Grade: *Sahih* (authentic) according to Al-Albani

Juwairiya reported: The Prophet, peace and blessings be upon him, came out from her apartment as she was performing the dawn prayer. He returned in the forenoon and found her sitting there. The Prophet said, "**Are you in the same position as I left you?**" She said yes. The Prophet said, "**I recited four words three times after I left you. If these are to be weighed against all you have recited since the morning, these words will be heavier. They are: Glory and praise to Allah as many as the numbers of His creation, in according with His pleasure, as the weight of the Throne, and as the ink for recording His words.**"Source: Sahih Muslim 2726 Grade: *Sahih* (authentic) according to Imam Muslim

Ubadah ibn As-Samit reported: We pledged allegiance to the Messenger of Allah, peace and blessings be upon him, pledging to listen and obey in hardship and in ease, in pleasure and displeasure even if someone is wrongly favored over us, and pledging not to dispute the rule of

those in authority and that we should speak the truth wherever we are and not to fear those who blame us regarding Allah.Source: Sahih Muslim 1709 Grade: *Sahih* (authentic) according to Imam Muslim

Al-Qurtubi reported: Some scholars gave permission to initiate greetings of peace with the unbelievers. It was said to Sufyan bin Uyainah, "Do you give permission to greet an unbeliever with peace?" Sufyan said, "Yes, for Allah the Exalted said: **Allah does not forbid you from those who do not fight you in religion nor expel you from your homes that you be righteous and fair to them. Verily, Allah loves those who are just**." (60:8) Sufyan added, "Allah said: **There has come to you the best example in Abraham**, (60:4) and Abraham said to his father: **Peace be upon you.**" (19:47)Source: Tafseer Al-Qurtubi, verse 19:41

Abdullah ibn Mas'ud reported: He stood upon a platform and he grabbed his tongue and he said, "O tongue! Speak goodness and be rewarded, or remain silent and be safe before you are regretful." Then he said: I heard the Messenger of Allah, peace and blessings be upon him, say, "**Most of the sins of the children of Adam are on their tongues.**"[At-Tabarani, Mu'jam Al-Kabeer, Number 10300, *Sahih*]

Anas ibn Malik reported: The Messenger of Allah, peace and blessings be upon him, said three times, "**May Allah have mercy on a person who spoke rightly and was rewarded, or who was silent and remained safe.**"Source: Shu'b Al-Iman Al-Bayhaqi 4579

Abu Huraira reported: The Messenger of Allah, peace and blessings be upon him, said, "**The basis of reasoning, after faith in Allah, is loving kindness toward the people.**"Source: At-Tabarani, Al-Mu'jam Al-Awsat, Number 6067

Abu Huraira reported: The Messenger of Allah, peace and blessings be upon him, said, "**Whoever believes in Allah and the Last Day, let him not harm his neighbor. Whoever believes in Allah and the Last Day, let him honor his guest. Whoever believes in Allah and the Last Day, let him speak goodness or remain silent.**"Source: Sahih Muslim 47

Ibn Mas'ud reported: The Prophet, peace and blessings be upon him, said, "**During the night journey, I met with Abraham, Moses, and Jesus and they were discussing the matter of the Hour. Their matter was referred to Abraham, who said, "I have no knowledge about it." So the matter was referred to Moses, who said, "I have no knowledge about it." So the matter was referred to Jesus, who said, "As for the conditions of the Hour, no one knows them but Allah. My Lord the Exalted has entrusted me that the False Messiah will appear and I will have with me two rods. When he sees me, he will melt away just as lead is melted in fire. Allah will destroy him to the point that the rock and the tree will say: O Muslims, beneath me is an unbeliever, so come slay him. Thus, Allah will destroy them and the people will return to their lands and their countries. When that happens, the nations of Gog and Magog will appear, eating and drinking everything in their lands. They will not come upon anything but that they will devour it and they will not pass by any water but that they will consume it. The people will complain to me about them, so I will supplicate to Allah and He will destroy them until their stench fills the earth. Then Allah will send rain which will wash their bodies into the sea. My Lord the Exalted has entrusted me that when all of this happens, the Hour is indeed near just as a women is ready to give birth; her family does not know when she will give birth but it could be any day or night.**"[Musnad Ahmad, Number 3546, *Sahih*]

Abu Huraira reported: The Messenger of Allah, peace and blessings be upon him, said, "**By Allah, the son of Mary will descend as a just ruler. He will abolish the cross, kill the swine, and annul the tribute, but he will leave the she-camel such that no one collects from it. He will cause rancor, hatred, and envy to disappear, and he will call people to give their wealth in charity but no one will need it.**"Source: Sahih Muslim 155

Prophet said, "By Allah, you must enjoin good and forbid evil and seize the hand of the oppressor and make him follow the truth and restrict him to what is just."Source: Sunan Abu Dawud 4336

"God is Kind and likes kindness in all things."Reporter: Hadhrat Ayeshah (r) Source: Bukhari/Muslim (reported in Riyadhus Saleheen,#633); Sunan Ibn Majah, #3684
**The people will be resurrected
(and judged) according to their intentions."**Reporter: Hadhrat Aishah (r) Source: Sahih al-Bukhari, Vol. 3, Book of Fasting, Chapter 6, p. 69

**"The best among you are those
who have the best manners and character.""**Reporter: Hadhrat Abdullah ibn Amr (r) Source: Sahih al-Bukhari, Vol. 8: #56b

"A person who goes in search of knowledge, he is in the path of God and he remains so till he returns."Reporter: Hadhrat Anas (r) Source: Sunan at-Tirmizi, Vol. 4, #2656

"Hell lies hidden behind evil (worldly desires) and paradise is screened behind hard labor."Reporter: Hadhrat Abu Hurairah (r) Source: Sahih al-Bukhari, Vol. 8, #494

"Paradise is closer to you than your shoelace, and so is the (Hell) Fire."Reporter: Hadhrat Ibn Mas'ud Source: Sahih al-Bukhari, Vol. 8, #495

"The world is prison for the believers and paradise for the disbelievers." Reporter: Hadhrat Abu Hurairah (r) Source: Sahih Muslim, Vol. 4, #7058

"To spend one morning or evening in the cause of God is better than the world and whatever is in the world." Reporter: Hadhrat Anas bin Malik Source: Sahih al-Bukhari, Vol. 4, #50

Surah 19 - Maryam MARY

019.001 Kaf, Ha, Ya, 'Ain, Sad. 019.002 (This is) a recital of the Mercy of thy Lord to His servant Zakariya. 019.003 Behold! he cried to his Lord in secret, 019.004 Praying: "O my Lord! infirm indeed are my bones, and the hair of my head doth glisten with grey: but never am I unblest, O my Lord, in my prayer to Thee! 019.005 "Now I fear (what) my relatives (and colleagues) (will do) after me: but my wife is barren: so give me an heir as from Thyself,-

019.006 "(One that) will (truly) represent me, and represent the posterity of Jacob; and make him, O my Lord! one with whom Thou art well-pleased!" 019.007 (His prayer was answered): "O Zakariya! We give thee good news of a son: His name shall be Yahya: on none by that name have We conferred distinction before." 019.008 He said: "O my Lord! How shall I have a son, when my wife is barren and I have grown quite decrepit from old age?" 019.009 He said: "So (it will be) thy Lord saith, 'that is easy for Me: I did indeed create thee before, when thou hadst been nothing!'" 019.010 (Zakariya) said: "O my Lord! give me a Sign." "Thy Sign," was the answer, "Shall be that thou shalt speak to no man for three nights, although thou art not dumb." 019.011 So Zakariya came out to his people from his chamber: He told them by signs to celebrate God's praises in the morning and in the evening. 019.012 (To his son came the command): "O Yahya! take hold of the Book with might": and We gave him Wisdom even as a youth, 019.013 And pity (for all creatures) as from Us, and purity: He was devout, 019.014 And kind to his parents, and he was not overbearing or rebellious. 019.015 So Peace on him the day he was born, the day that he dies, and the day that he will be raised up to life (again)! 019.016 Relate in the Book (the story of) Mary, when she withdrew from her family to a place in the East. 019.017 She placed a screen (to screen herself) from them; then We sent to her our angel, and he appeared before her as a man in all respects. 019.018 She said: "I seek refuge from thee to (God) Most Gracious: (come not near) if thou dost fear God." 019.019 He said: "Nay, I am only a messenger from thy Lord, (to announce) to thee the gift of a holy son. 019.020 She said: "How shall I have a son, seeing that no man has touched me, and I am not unchaste?" 019.021 He said: "So (it will be): Thy Lord saith, 'that is easy for Me: and (We wish) to appoint him as a Sign unto men and a Mercy from Us':It is a matter (so) decreed." 019.022 So she conceived him, and she retired with him to a remote place. 019.023 And the pains of childbirth drove her to the trunk of a palm-tree: She cried (in her anguish): "Ah! would that I had died before this! would that I had been a thing forgotten and out of sight!" 019.024 But (a voice) cried to her from beneath the (palm-tree): "Grieve not! for thy Lord hath provided a rivulet beneath thee; 019.025 "And shake towards thyself the trunk of the palm-tree: It will let fall fresh ripe dates upon thee. 019.026 "So eat and drink and cool (thine) eye. And if thou dost see any man, say, 'I have vowed a fast to (God) Most Gracious, and this day will I enter into not talk with any human being'" 019.027 At length she brought the (babe) to her people, carrying him (in her arms). They said: "O Mary! truly an amazing thing hast thou brought! 019.028 "O sister of Aaron! Thy father was not a man of evil, nor thy mother a woman unchaste!" 019.029 But she pointed to the babe. They said: "How can we talk to one who is a child in the cradle?" 019.030 He said: "I am indeed a servant of God: He hath given me revelation and made me a prophet; 019.031 "And He hath made me blessed wheresoever I be, and hath enjoined on me Prayer and Charity as long as I live; 019.032 "(He) hath made me kind to my mother, and not overbearing or miserable; 019.033 "So peace is on me the day I was born, the day that I die, and the day that I shall be raised up to life (again)"! 019.034 Such (was) Jesus the son of Mary: (it is) a statement of truth, about which they (vainly) dispute. 019.035 It is not befitting to (the majesty of) God that He should beget a son. Glory be to Him! when He determines a matter, He only says to it, "Be", and it is. 019.036 Verily God is my Lord and your Lord: Him therefore serve ye: this is a Way that is straight. 019.037 But the sects differ among themselves: and woe to the unbelievers because of the (coming) Judgment of a Momentous Day! 019.038 How plainly will they see and hear, the Day that they will appear before Us! but the unjust today are in error manifest! 019.039 But warn them of the Day of Distress, when the matter will be determined: for (behold,) they are negligent and they do not believe! 019.040 It is We Who will inherit the earth, and all beings thereon: to Us will they all be returned. 019.041 (Also) mention in the Book (the story of) Abraham: He was a man of Truth, a prophet. 019.042 Behold, he said to his father: "O my father! why worship that which heareth not and seeth not, and can profit thee nothing? 019.043 "O my father! to me hath come knowledge which hath not reached thee: so follow me: I will guide thee to a way that is even and straight. 019.044 "O my father! serve not Satan: for Satan is a rebel against (God) Most Gracious. 019.045 "O my father! I fear lest a Penalty afflict thee from (God) Most Gracious, so that thou become to Satan a friend." 019.046 (The father) replied: "Dost thou hate my gods, O Abraham? If thou forbear not, I will indeed stone thee: Now get away from me for a good long while!" 019.047 Abraham said: "Peace be on thee: I will pray to my Lord for thy forgiveness: for He is to me Most Gracious. 019.048 "And I will turn away from you (all) and from those whom ye invoke besides God: I will call on my Lord: perhaps, by my prayer to my Lord, I shall be not unblest." 019.049 When he had turned away from them and from those whom they worshipped besides God, We bestowed on him Isaac and Jacob, and each one of them We made a prophet. 019.050 And We bestowed of Our Mercy on them, and We granted them lofty honour on the tongue of truth. 019.051 Also mention in the Book (the story of) Moses: for he was specially chosen, and he was a messenger (and) a prophet. 019.052 And we called him from the right side of Mount (Sinai), and made him draw near to Us, for mystic (converse). 019.053 And, out of Our Mercy, We gave him his brother Aaron, (also) a prophet. 019.054 Also mention in the Book (the story of) Isma'il: He was (strictly) true to what he promised, and he was a messenger (and) a prophet. 019.055 He used to enjoin on his people Prayer and Charity, and he was most acceptable in the sight of his Lord. 019.056 Also mention in the Book the case of Idris: He was a man of truth (and sincerity), (and) a prophet: 019.057 And We raised him to a lofty station. 019.058 Those were some of the prophets on whom God did bestow His Grace,- of the posterity of Adam, and of those who We carried (in the Ark) with Noah, and of the posterity of Abraham and Israel of those whom We guided and chose. Whenever the Signs of (God) Most Gracious were rehearsed to them, they would fall down in prostrate adoration and in tears. 019.059 But after them there followed a posterity who missed prayers and followed after lusts soon, then, will they face Destruction,- 019.060 Except those who repent and believe, and work righteousness: for these will enter the Garden and will not be wronged in the least,- 019.061 Gardens of Eternity, those which (God) Most Gracious has promised to His servants in the Unseen: for His promise must (necessarily) come to pass. 019.062 They will not there hear any vain discourse, but only salutations of Peace: And they will have therein their sustenance, morning and evening. 019.063 Such is the Garden which We give as an inheritance to those of Our servants who guard against Evil. 019.064 (The angels say:) "We descend not but by command of thy Lord: to Him belongeth what is before us and what is behind us, and what is between: and thy Lord never doth forget,- 019.065 "Lord of the heavens and of the earth, and of all that is between them; so worship Him, and be constant and patient in His worship:

knowest thou of any who is worthy of the same Name as He?" 019.066 Man says: "What! When I am dead, shall I then be raised up alive?" 019.067 But does not man call to mind that We created him before out of nothing? 019.068 So, by thy Lord, without doubt, We shall gather them together, and (also) the Evil Ones (with them); then shall We bring them forth on their knees round about Hell; 019.069 Then shall We certainly drag out from every sect all those who were worst in obstinate rebellion against (God) Most Gracious. 019.070 And certainly We know best those who are most worthy of being burned therein. 019.071 Not one of you but will pass over it: this is, with thy Lord, a Decree which must be accomplished. 019.072 But We shall save those who guarded against evil, and We shall leave the wrong-doers therein, (humbled) to their knees. 019.073 When Our Clear Signs are rehearsed to them, the Unbelievers say to those who believe, "Which of the two sides is best in point of position? Which makes the best show in council?" 019.074 But how many (countless) generations before them have we destroyed, who were even better in equipment and in glitter to the eye? 019.075 Say: "If any men go astray, (God) Most Gracious extends (the rope) to them, until, when they see the warning of God (being fulfilled) - either in punishment or in (the approach of) the Hour,- they will at length realise who is worst in position, and (who) weaker in forces! 019.076 "And God doth advance in guidance those who seek guidance: and the things that endure, Good Deeds, are best in the sight of thy Lord, as rewards, and best in respect of (their) eventual return." 019.077 Hast thou then seen the (sort of) man who rejects Our Signs, yet says: "I shall certainly be given wealth and children?" 019.078 Has he penetrated to the Unseen, or has he taken a contract with (God) Most Gracious? 019.079 Nay! We shall record what he says, and We shall add and add to his punishment. 019.080 To Us shall return all that he talks of and he shall appear before Us bare and alone. 019.081 And they have taken (for worship) gods other than God, to give them power and glory! 019.082 Instead, they shall reject their worship, and become adversaries against them. 019.083 Seest thou not that We have set the Evil Ones on against the unbelievers, to incite them with fury? 019.084 So make no haste against them, for We but count out to them a (limited) number (of days). 019.085 The day We shall gather the righteous to (God) Most Gracious, like a band presented before a king for honours, 019.086 And We shall drive the sinners to Hell, like thirsty cattle driven down to water,- 019.087 None shall have the power of intercession, but such a one as has received permission (or promise) from (God) Most Gracious. 019.088 They say: "(God) Most Gracious has begotten a son!" 019.089 Indeed ye have put forth a thing most monstrous! 019.090 As if the skies are ready to burst, the earth to split asunder, and the mountains to fall down in utter ruin. 019.091 That they should invoke a son for (God) Most Gracious. 019.092 For it is not consonant with the majesty of (God) Most Gracious that He should beget a son. 019.093 Not one of the beings in the heavens and the earth but must come to (God) Most Gracious as a servant. 019.094 He does take an account of them (all), and hath numbered them (all) exactly. 019.095 And everyone of them will come to Him singly on the Day of Judgment. 019.096 On those who believe and work deeds of righteousness, will (God) Most Gracious bestow love. 019.097 So have We made the (Qur'an) easy in thine own tongue, that with it thou mayest give Glad Tidings to the righteous, and warnings to people given to contention. 019.098 But how many (countless) generations before them have We destroyed? Canst thou find a single one of them (now) or hear (so much as) a whisper of them?Al-Quran

DID ISLAM EXIST BEFORE MUHAMMAD?

God does not born or die he is forever. Jesus, Moses, Mohammad & all other people of Bible, Quran &Torah were great messengers prophets of god not sons of god they were created by 1 true god, creator, Allah. So any creation can't be the 1 creator Allah. So they were messengers, prophets of god. How can creator be part of what he has created Himself!!!So he is not part of any creation again he is not a creation & has no partners no father ,mother, daughter ,son, brother, sister ,wife & no gender simply unique beyond comparable & 1 & 1 only. From Adam to Jesus god sent his messages for every generation or period of time but it was always destroyed by mankind & the devils conspiracy to take mankind towards hell. Because all previous books were massed up by humans Allah sent his last messenger not son or god, but messenger Mohammad & sent him Quran & it's messages to guide humans towards Allah & heaven. Allah has promised to Keep Quran same until the Day of Judgment & challenged humans to create another accurate book like Quran & said if you can't then surrender to your lord (the only way of peace&heaven).Majority of things science has discovered until now 80% of Quran had all those undiscovered answers from the last 1400years when science didn't have any answers. The other 20% answer was & is in Quran. Maybe it will take science another 1400years to find it. All 100% answers are in Quran. Science can't prove a single verse of Quran wrong. If you do a research on Quran, bible and science you will find facts. Facts are stranger than fiction. In the bible it says Jesus bowed his head on floor just like Muslims bow their head on floor while praying .You should do research on bible, Quran &science if you believe in god so you can find facts on Islam. If I teach a parrot a message & send it to someone & parrot tells the message to that person and leaves & that person starts saying that parrot is my son that would make no sense, because that was my messenger not son. Jesus was taken up alive &after that people started calling him son of god. He came to establish Islam & was a messenger of 1 god. Christianity started after Jesus was gone, Jesus will comeback & die as a human& Muslim. Quran is the only accurate 100% words of god &word of god can't have errors then it would not be word of god & according to science bibles & Torahs has many errors but they can't prove a verse in Quran wrong. Muslims believe there is no god but Allah & Prophet Mohammad is the last & final prophet & messenger of Allah.

Adam, Abraham ,Noah, Moses ,Jesus , Muhammad were all messengers & prophets of 1 God Allah so Islam is the 1st religion & it's the last religion because God is Allah & God is forever so is God's religion which is only Islam & it is also forever. Finally Islam always existed even before Adam, Abraham ,Noah, Moses ,Jesus & Muhammad because it's the only true religion from God Allah.

ISA"Jesus", the prophet of Islam

- Introduction
- MARYAM, THEMOTHER OF ^ISA(Jesus)
- THE BIRTH OF ^ISA(Jesus)
- EARLY LIFE OF PROPHET ^ISA(Jesus)
- THEREVELATION OF PROPHETHOOD
- THE INJIL(BIBLE)
- THEASCENSION OF PROPHET ^ISA(Jesus)
- PROPHET ^ISA'S(Jesus) DESCENT TO EARTH
- CONCLUSION

Introduction

Allah sent many messengers to the humans as a mercy from Him. *Allah* sent them all to teach the people what is the correct and acceptable worship of *Allah*--their Creator and the Creator of everything. All the prophets of *Allah*, the first of whom was *Adam* and the last of whom is *Muhammad*, came with one Religion--*Islam,* one creed--the belief in the Oneness of *Allah*. They all taught that *Allah* is attributed with all the perfect attributes and that He does not resemble any of His creations. They taught what *Allah* ordered us to perform with and refrain from in this life. They taught there is the Judgment Day in which each one of us will be judged as to whether or not we fulfilled our obligations in this life. None of them taught their people what contradicts the belief in the Oneness of *Allah*. Each one of them ordered their followers to believe in the rest of the prophets. *Imam al-Bukhariyy* related that Prophet *Muhammad, sallallahu ^alayhi wa sallam*, said:

which means:<< The prophets are like brothers from the same father with different mothers. Their Religion is one although their *Shari^ah* (rules of the Religion) differed. I am the most deserving of Prophet *^Isa*. There was no other prophet between us.>>

Allah revealed Prophet *^Isa* (Jesus) as the messenger before Prophet *Muhammad*. He was one of the five best messengers of *Allah*, called *Ulul-^Azm*, those with the highest status, who were the most patient. He was *^Isa*, the son of *Maryam*, the daughter of *^Imran*, from the sons of Israel. Prophet *^Isa*, as all the prophets, was truthful in what he conveyed from *Allah*, and although today we follow the *Shari^ah* of Prophet *Muhammad*, Muslims respect, love, and believe in *^Isa* and in his prophethood.

MARYAM, THE MOTHER OF ^ISA *(Jesus)*

Maryam (Mary), the mother of *^Isa*, was a pious Muslim woman from the offspring of Israel during the time of Prophet *Zakariyya*. Prophet *Zakariyya* was a prophet of *Allah* revealed to convey to the people to follow the *Shari^ah* revealed to Prophet *Musa*. In the *Qur'an* there is a chapter named *Maryam* referring to *Maryam* (Mary), the mother of *^Isa*. This chapter talks about *Maryam:* her birth, her story, and the birth of Prophet *^Isa*, and other things.

Maryam's mother conceived and delivered Maryam when she was an old woman, at an age when women usually can no longer have babies. One day *Maryam's* mother saw a bird feeding its young and she longed for a baby herself. She made a supplication to *Allah* to bless her with a child and vowed that she would make him a servant for the Holy House in Jerusalem, dedicated for worship, because she thought the child would be male. *Allah* answered her supplication and *Maryam's* mother conceived and delivered a baby girl. She named her "*Maryam*" and asked *Allah* to protect her and her offspring from evil.

Since *Maryam's* father had died, Prophet *Zakariyya* (who was the husband of *Maryam's* sister) became *Maryam's* guardian. From him, *Maryam* learned the Religion. She grew up as a righteous, pure, and pious Muslim woman worshipping *Allah* and endeavoring greatly in performing obedience to Him. Before she turned fourteen (14) years old, Maryam was a *waliyyah* (a very pious woman with a special status). She became the best of the women in the world. It is mentioned in the *Qur'an* that the angels said *Allah* chose *Maryam* and preferred her to the other women of the world. (*Al ^Imran*, 42-43).

THE BIRTH OF ^ISA (Jesus)

Ibn Jarir and others narrated that one day *Maryam* ran out of water. She asked her cousin, *Yusuf*, the son of *Ya^qub* to go with her to get some. He declined, saying he had his sufficiency for that day, so *Maryam* went to fetch water alone. There, she found *Jibril*, whom *Allah* had sent to her in the shape of a man. Thinking he was a human who might harm her, she asked refuge with *Allah* from him. *Jibril* told her, "I am the Messenger of your Lord to you. I was sent to give you a pious child who is pure from sins." *Maryam* told him, "How would I have a son? I have no husband, and I am not an adulterer or a fornicator." *Jibril* told her, "Creating a son without a father is an easy matter to *Allah*. *Allah* will make him a sign for the people and an indication of the Power of *Allah*. He will send him as a mercy from Him and an endowment to the one who follows him and believes in him. Creating him is a matter *Allah* willed and destined, so it will not be blocked or changed."

Jibril blew the soul of ^*Isa* into *Maryam* and ^*Isa's* soul entered into her womb. *Maryam* became pregnant with ^*Isa*, peace be upon him. There is a difference of opinion as to the term of her pregnancy, some said nine months, some said eight, and some said other than that. However, when the signs of pregnancy became apparent on her, her cousin, *Yusuf* the Carpenter, was disturbed and did not know how to interpret that matter. If he wanted to accuse her he would remember how pious she was. If he wanted to declare her innocence, he would see the signs of pregnancy. So he decided to open the subject with her. He asked her, "Tell me, would plants grow without seeds? Would trees grow without rainfall? Would there be a child without a male?" To all these questions *Maryam* said "Yes." Then she asked him, "Did you not know *Allah* made the plants emerge without seeds the day He created them? Did you not know *Allah* created the trees the first time without rain? Did you not know *Allah* created *Adam* and *Hawwa'* (Eve) without a father or a mother?" *Yusuf* knew all these things and when she responded in this way, he felt assured of her innocence and that this was something special given to her by *Allah*.

When the signs of her pregnancy became apparent, *Maryam* went away from her people. The pangs of birth led her to the trunk of a dead palm tree. Out of her shyness from the people, and fearing they would accuse her of having done something ugly, she wished she was dead and not a trace of her could be found. *Jibril* called to her, comforting her. He told her *Allah* made a small river run under her from which she could drink, and should she shake the trunk of the dead palm tree next to her, it would turn green and moist dates would fall down from which she could eat and be nourished. *Jibril* told her when she faces her people with her son to tell anyone who questions her about him that she had made a vow not to talk to any human for that day. That day, *Maryam* gave birth to her son, ^*Isa*, peace be upon him. Forty (40) days later she carried him back to her people. They accused her of having fornicated. In response, Maryam pointed to her son, meaning to tell them to talk to him. They were angered at this and thought she was mocking them by asking them to speak with a 40-day old baby lying in a small cradle. At this, *Allah* made ^*Isa* speak. He said:

which are verses 30-33 of *Surat Maryam* and mean: [I am a slave of *Allah*. He will reveal the Book to me and make me a prophet. He blessed me wherever I am. In the rules revealed to me there will be a special attention given to Prayers and *Zakat*. *Allah* predestined that I will be kind to my mother and not a tyrant with a bad ending. Peace was on me the day I was born. Peace will be on me on the day I will die and on the day I am raised alive again.]

When *Maryam's* people heard that, they refrained from harming her or Prophet *Zakariyya*, about whom they had made ugly accusations. After Baby ^*Isa* spoke these words, he did not speak again until he became at an age when children normally begin to speak. ^*Isa's* speaking from the cradle was a preparation and a sign of his creed and coming prophethood, when he would call the people to believe in *Allah*, the One Who does not have a partner and to believe in the message of ^*Isa*--that he was the slave and messenger of *Allah*. The first words he spoke were, "I am a slave of *Allah*."

EARLY LIFE OF PROPHET ^*ISA* (Jesus)

Lady *Maryam* took ^*Isa* to Egypt where they stayed for a period of time. Then they returned to the countries of *ash-Sham*--to a city known as *an-Nasirah*. ^*Isa*, peace be upon him, studied the Torah in the schools and memorized it. He spoke Syriac, the language of the people of Palestine at that time, and the language in which the Heavenly Book, called the *Injil*, was revealed to him. He was a pious worshipper of *Allah*, following the rules of the Torah revealed to Prophet *Musa*.

THE REVELATION OF PROPHETHOOD

Allah sent the Revelation of Prophethood to ^*Isa* when he was thirty years old. *Allah* revealed to him new laws which abrogated some of the laws revealed to Prophet *Musa*. Prophet ^*Isa* conveyed the revelation to the people and called them to believe in his message.

Prophet ^*Isa*, like all the prophets of *Allah*, performed miracles. *Allah* sent all the prophets with miracles as a proof to their prophethood, so the people would witness, know about them, and believe in their prophethood. Many of Prophet ^*Isa's* miracles were in curing illnesses, to be a stronger proof of his truthfulness, since the people at his time were famous for being knowledgeable in the field of medicine. Prophet ^*Isa* cured those with seemingly incurable illnesses. Prophet ^*Isa* cured a man inflicted with leprosy. He put his honorable hand on the face of a man who was born blind and cured his sight. Once Prophet ^*Isa* supplicated to *Allah* to bring back to life one person who had died and was being carried to the burial place, and *Allah* brought this person back to life.

Prophet ^Isa had other kinds of miracles also. He formed the shape of bats from clay and then they would fly away a distance. One of the miracles of ^*Isa* is mentioned in the *Qur'an* in *Surat al-Ma'idah*, Verses 112-114, which tells about one time when Prophet ^*Isa* and the people who were with him reached to a place where there was not enough food for all the people with him. The students of ^*Isa* asked him to supplicate *Allah* for food which would come down on them from the sky. ^*Isa* made supplication to *Allah* and the angels brought down the food on a piece of material before the eyes of the people. Hundreds and hundreds of people ate from that food, and there was no sign the food had diminished in quantity. This miracle increased the belief of the believers. The blasphemers however, claimed ^*Isa* had performer sorcery on their eyes.

After his revelation, Prophet ^*Isa* lived on earth for about three years. He used to travel from place to place calling people to the proper worship of *Allah*. He was so detached from the worldly matters that he did not worry that he did not have a house to return to at night. He used to sleep wherever the night would fall on him, whether he was in an open land or in a sheltered place. He wore clothing made out of unwoven wool. He ate from the raw plants of the earth, without desiring to cook them. He did not marry or have children.

THE *INJIL(BIBLE)*

^*Isa* received a Heavenly Book, the *Injil*, which contained the *Shari^ah*, (rules of the Religion) revealed to him. In it was the prohibition of associating partners with *Allah*. In it was the prohibition to consume the usurious gain (*riba*), pig meat, blood, and the meat of animals not slaughtered properly. It contained the order to perform the Prayer (with bowing and prostration) twice a day. It had the order to fast (but other than the month of *Ramadan*), and the order to perform *taharah*. Prophet ^*Isa* came with a *Shari^ah* that contained making permissible some of the things which had been forbidden upon the children of Israel in the Torah. Although what is called "The Bible" today contains some true stories of Prophet ^*Isa*, it does not contain the true *Injil* which was revealed to him.

THE ASCENSION OF PROPHET ^*ISA(Jesus)*

When Prophet ^Isa was 33 years old, the blasphemers among the offspring of Israel plotted to kill him, but Allah saved him from their harm. Ibn AbiHatim and an-Nasa'iyy narrated from the route of Ibn ^Abbas that he said:

Prophet ^Isa was in session with twelve of his elite companions in a house. He told them that among them would be who would blaspheme in the future. Then he asked them, "Who among you would want to be made to look like me, be killed in my place, and be my companion in Paradise." The youngest among them stood up and said, "Me." Prophet ^Isa told him to sit, then repeated his same question. Again, the same young man said, "Me." Again, Prophet ^Isa told him to sit, then again asked the same question. After the same young man volunteered for the third time, Prophet ^Isa received the Revelation that this young man would be the one who would be made to look like him and killed instead of him. Prophet ^Isa was raised to the sky from an opening in the ceiling of the house. When the Jews came after Prophet ^Isa, they saw that young man, whom Allah made to look like ^Isa. They took him, thinking he was Prophet ^Isa, and crucified him.

It should be noted here there are two widespread false stories about this matter. In one, it is claimed that one of ^Isa's students was paid a great sum of money to lead those Jews to

^Isa however Allah made him look like ^Isa, so they though he was ^Isa and they crucified him. In another, it is said that the person killed in place of ^Isa was the leader of the Jews. Both of these stories are false.

After Prophet ^Isa was raised to the sky, his nation lived following his guidance, teaching, and methodology for two hundred (200) years. However, the nation of Prophet ^Isa did not remain steadfast to Islam. Three hundred (300) years after Prophet ^Isa was raised to the sky, those who were following the ones who had perverted the teachings of Prophet ^Isa became very numerous, and those who were truly following the Religion of Islam were few and weak. After some five hundred (500) years, none of the believing Muslims of ^Isa's nation were left. When Prophet Muhammad was revealed, he was the only Muslim worshipping only Allah from among the people of the earth.

PROPHET ^ISA'S (Jesus) DESCENT TO EARTH

Prophet ^Isa, peace be upon him, is still alive--in the second sky--worshipping Allah. He will descend to earth before the Day of Judgment and his descent will be one of the great signs of the nearing of that Day. Prophet Muhammad informed us ^Isa will descend to earth at a place on the eastern side of Damascus, with his hands on the wings of two angels. He will meet a group of Muslims getting ready to perform the Prayer, with the Mahdiyy as their Imam. The Mahdiyy will ask Prophet ^Isa to lead them in that prayer, however, ^Isa will ask the Mahdiyy to stand imam for them--as a sign that Prophet ^Isa will rule with the rules revealed to Prophet Muhammad. After this one time, ^Isa will lead the people in prayers because he has a higher status than the Mahdiyy.

After he descends, Prophet ^*Isa* will rule the earth with the *Shari^ah* of Prophet *Muhammad*, the *Shari^ah* Muslims are ordered to follow until the Judgment Day. He will break the cross, kill the pig, and abolish the *jizyah* (compulsory payment by the People of the Book to the Muslim state), because in the rules of Prophet *Muhammad* the *jizyah* is only applicable until the descent of ^*Isa*. He will kill the *Dajjal*, an ugly, evil blasphemer who claims himself as God, and who misleads many people to blaspheme. Prophet ^*Isa* will perform *Hajj* and travel to visit the grave of the Prophet to salute him, and to greet him by saying, "*As-salamu ^alaykum ya rasulAllah*", as narrated by *Abu Dawud at-Tayalisiyy* and others.

During his time, the people of *Ya'juj* and *Ma'juj* will appear and cause great destruction to the earth and devastation to the Muslims. Prophet ^*Isa* will take the believers to Mount *at-Tur* to supplicate *Allah* there to relieve them from these people. *Allah* will answer their *du^a'* and destroy all the people of *Ya'juj* and *Ma'juj*. After that, Prophet ^*Isa* will rule the Muslims and there will be a time

when peace, comfort, and safety will prevail. Prophet ^*Isa* will live for forty (40) years on earth after he descends. He will marry and have children. Then, he will die and be buried. ^*Adullah Ibn Salam* said, "It is written in the original Torah that Prophet ^*Isa* will be buried next to Prophet *Muhammad*" (in the chamber of Lady ^*A'ishah*.)

CONCLUSION

Prophet ^*Isa* was a messenger of *Allah* revealed to convey to the people the religion of *Islam* and to call them to worship *Allah*, their Creator. Muslims believe in his prophethood and in his truthfulness in conveying that message. Prophet ^*Isa* is alive now, living in the second heaven, worshipping *Allah*. He will return to earth before the Day of Judgment and will rule the world. Peace be upon this respected, honored and beloved Messenger of *Allah*.

Praise be to *Allah*, and *Allah* knows best.

Verse #33 of *SuratMaryam* means:

[Peace was on me the day I was born. Peace will be on me on the day I will die and on the day I am raised alive again.]

<u>Conclusion of the entire book</u>

He said: "I am indeed a servant of God: He hath given me revelation and made me a prophet; 019.031 "And He hath made me blessed wheresoever

I be, and hath enjoined on me Prayer and Charity as long as I live; 019.032 "(He) hath made me kind to my mother, and not overbearing or miserable; 019.033 "So peace is on me the day I was born, the day that I die, and the day that I shall be raised up to life (again)"! 019.034 Such (was) Jesus the son of Mary: (it is) a statement of truth, about which they (vainly) dispute. 019.035 It is not befitting to (the majesty of) God that He should beget a son. Glory be to Him! when He determines a matter, He only says to it,"Be",and it is. <u>***Al-Quran.***</u>

There is no God but Allah & Adam, Abraham, Noah, Moses, Jesus, Muhammad were all messengers & prophets of 1 God. The Quran is the final testament book of God's words only. The Quran proves God exists .Jesus was born without a father. There is no doubt in the evidences of history that Muhammad & Jesus existed & they were prophets of 1 true God Allah.

21. Had We sent down this Qur'an on a mountain, verily, thou wouldst have seen it humble itself and cleave asunder for fear of Allah. Such are the similitudes which We propound to men, that they may reflect. 22. Allah is He, than Whom there is no other god;- Who knows (all things) both secret and open; He, Most Gracious, Most Merciful. 23 .Allah is He, than Whom there is no other god;- the Sovereign, the Holy One, the Source of Peace (and Perfection), the Guardian of Faith, the Preserver of Safety, the Exalted in Might, the Irresistible, the Supreme: Glory to Allah! (High is He) above the partners they attribute to Him. 24 .He is Allah, the Creator, the Evolver, the Bestower of Forms (or Colours). To Him belong the Most Beautiful Names: whatever is in the heavens and on earth, doth declare His Praises and Glory: and He is the Exalted in Might, the Wise. {Al-Hashr- Al Quran}1. Praise be to Allah, to Whom belong all things in the heavens and on earth: to Him be Praise in the Hereafter: and He is Full of Wisdom, acquainted with all things. 2. He knows all that goes into the earth, and all that comes out thereof; all that comes down from the sky and all that ascends thereto and He is the Most Merciful, the Oft-Forgiving. 3 .The Unbelievers say, "Never to us will come the Hour": Say, "Nay! but most surely, by my Lord, it will come upon you;- by Him Who knows the unseen,- from Whom is not hidden the least little atom in the heavens or on earth: Nor is there anything less than that, or greater, but is in the Record Perspicuous:

4 .That He may reward those who believe and work deeds of righteousness: for such is Forgiveness and a Sustenance Most Generous." 5 .But those who strive against Our Signs, to frustrate them,- for such will be a Penalty,- a Punishment most humiliating. 6 .And those to whom knowledge has come see that the (Revelation) sent down to thee from thy Lord - that is the Truth, and that it guides to the Path of the Exalted (in might), Worthy of all praise. (Saba 34 Al-Quran)

Surah 3. The Family Of 'Imran, The House Of 'Imran(Quran) 1. A. L. M. 2. Allah. There is no god but He,-the Living, the Self-Subsisting, Eternal. 3. It is He Who sent down to thee (step by step), in truth, the Book, confirming what went before it; and He sent down the Law (of Moses) and the Gospel (of Jesus) before this, as a guide to mankind, and He sent down the criterion (of judgment between right and wrong). 4. Then those who reject Faith in the Signs of Allah will suffer the severest penalty, and Allah is Exalted in Might, Lord of Retribution. 5. From Allah, verily nothing is hidden on earth or in the heavens. 6. He it is Who shapes you in the wombs as He pleases. There is no god but He, the Exalted in Might, the

Wise. 7. He it is Who has sent down to thee the Book: In it are verses basic or fundamental (of established meaning); they are the foundation of the Book: others are allegorical. But those in whose hearts is perversity follow the part thereof that is allegorical, seeking discord, and searching for its hidden meanings, but no one knows its hidden meanings except Allah. And those who are firmly grounded in knowledge say: "We believe in the Book; the whole of it is from our Lord:" and none will grasp the Message except men of understanding. 8. "Our Lord!" (they say), "Let not our hearts deviate now after Thou hast guided us, but grant us mercy from Thine own Presence; for Thou art the Grantor of bounties without measure. 9. "Our Lord! Thou art He that will gather mankind Together against a day about which there is no doubt; for Allah never fails in His promise." 10. Those who reject Faith,- neither their possessions nor their (numerous) progeny will avail them aught against Allah. They are themselves but fuel for the Fire.

{Surah Baqarah Quran}284. To Allah belongeth all that is in the heavens and on earth. Whether ye show what is in your minds or conceal it, Allah Calleth you to account for it. He forgiveth whom He pleaseth, and punisheth whom He pleaseth, for Allah hath power over all things. 285. The Messenger believeth in what hath been revealed to him from his Lord, as do the men of faith. Each one (of them) believeth in Allah, His angels, His books, and His apostles. "We make no distinction (they say) between one and another of His apostles." And they say: "We hear, and we obey: (We seek) Thy forgiveness, our Lord, and to Thee is the end of all journeys." 286. On no soul doth Allah Place a burden greater than it can bear. It gets every good that it earns, and it suffers every ill that it earns. (Pray:) "Our Lord! Condemn us not if we forget or fall into error; our Lord! Lay not on us a burden Like that which Thou didst lay on those before us; Our Lord! Lay not on us a burden greater than we have strength to bear. Blot out our sins, and grant us forgiveness. Have mercy on us. Thou art our Protector; Help us against those who stand against faith."

(ONLY GOD IS ALL KNOWN & SATAN,HUMANS,ANGELS,JINNS ARE NOT ALL KNOWN.THE QURAN'S INFORMATION IS ACCURATE BECAUSE IT'S THE FINAL,LAST BOOK OF THE TRUE1GOD LORD ALLAH.)

<u>**Allah (swt) Says**</u> **: "Invite to the Way of your Lord (i.e. Islam) with wisdom (i.e. with the Divine Revelation and the Qur'an) and fair preaching, and argue with them in a way that is better. Truly, your Lord knows best who has gone astray from His Path, and He is the Best Aware of those who are guided."[Quran 16:125]** <u>**Allah also says**</u> **'"Who is better in speech than one who calls to Allah, works righteousness, and says: I am of those who bow in submission?" (Quran 41:33)** <u>**Prophet Muhammad (PBUH) said:**</u>**"If Allah guides a person through you, it is better for you than all that is on the earth." (Bukhari No. 2783 & Muslim No. 2406).Convey (my teachings) to the people even if it were a single sentence" (Sahih Bukhari, Vol.4, Hadith 667)**

"Therefore listen not to the Unbelievers, but strive against them with the utmost strenuousness, with the (Qur'an)". 25.52 Quran

Yet do they worship, besides Allah, things that can neither profit them nor harm them: and the disbeliever is a helper (of Evil), against his own Lord! 25.55 Quran

And I have sent you only as a giver of good news and as a warner. 25.56

Say: "No reward do I ask of you for it but this: that each one who will may take a (straight) Path to his Allah." *25.57 Al-Quran*

"Verily, those who conceal the clear proofs, evidences and the guidance, which We have sent down, after We have made it clear for the people in the Book, they are the ones cursed by Allah and cursed by the cursers."(Quran, al-Baqarah: 159) ***Prophet Muhammad (PBUH) said: "For Allah to guide one man through you is better for***

you than all that the sun has shined over".
The Prophet (PBUH) has said: "Whoever guides [another] to a good deed will get a reward similar to the one who performs it."
[Saheeh Muslim]

SOME BOOKS BY MR.FAISAL FAHIM

1((The History, Biographies, Science, Evidences And The Truth About Moses, Jesus,Muhammad)

2(The God Delusion VS. The Bible,The Quran and Science)

THESE BOOK ARE AVAILABLE ON WWW.AMAZON.COM

Made in the USA
Monee, IL
22 August 2023